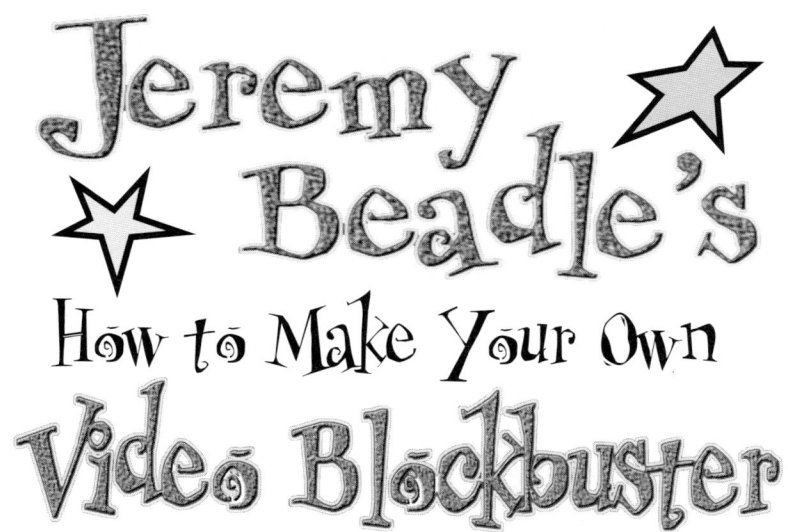

Jeremy Beadle's
How to Make Your Own
Video Blockbuster

with Mark Leigh and Mike Lepine

The simplest guide ever to making fun videos at home and on holiday

HEADLINE

First published in 1998

by HEADLINE BOOK PUBLISHING

10 9 8 7 6 5 4 3 2 1

ISBN 0 7472 7634 X

Designed by Design/Section, Frome

Typeset by Letterpart Limited, Reigate, Surrey

Printed and bound in Italy by Canale & C.S.p.A.

HEADLINE BOOK PUBLISHING

A division of Hodder Headline PLC

338 Euston Road

London NW1 3BH

Contents

Making Blockbusters Is Fun!

If you own a camcorder, the chances are you're only using it to record your children growing up, taping your holidays, the occasional wedding and little else . . .

> *Have a go.*
> *Anybody can do it*
> **Alan Parker, director of *Bugsy Malone*,**
> ***Fame* and *The Commitments***

> *If you can drive a*
> *car, you can direct*
> *a movie*
> **John Landis, director of *An American***
> ***Werewolf in London*, *Blues Brothers***
> **and *Trading Places***

That's a shame, because you really could be having a lot of fun with your camcorder, making your own comedy Blockbusters starring your friends and family – produced and directed by you!

You could be making videos you and your family will treasure forever, and enjoying a new hobby that stimulates your mind, gets you off the sofa and out with your mates – and stretches your imagination. You could be discovering talents you never knew you had. You could be the next Steven Spielberg.

Above all, making your own Video Blockbuster is great fun. It can be a real laugh and – once you've got your own camcorder – it can be a cheap hobby as well.

The purpose of *How to Make Your Own Video Blockbuster* is to get you started. Everything you need to know is in here and I've tried to make it all as straightforward and simple as possible. I'll take you step by step through each part of the process, with lots of common-sense hints and tips and secret tricks of the trade rather than boring, in-depth technical details. I hate jargon and I expect you do too.

This is really more an ideas book than a technical manual. The emphasis is firmly on helping you to come up with a good idea to start with. With one good idea you can make a wonderful home Blockbuster regardless of the equipment you own or the money you've got to spend. I've included lots of examples and suggestions. Use them to get you started or say to yourself, 'Crikey, Jeremy, I can do better than that!' and develop your own ideas, because you're probably right!

Once you've made your first couple of Blockbusters, you could easily find yourself getting addicted to it. You'll want to find out

more about different techniques, especially editing. We had intended to make the book a bit more technical, but when the editor saw the size of the original manuscript she took a cue from the subject matter and shouted, 'Cut!' There are, however, a number of good books on video making to help you hone your technical skills further; there are also video clubs up and down the country you can join. The sky's the limit – and you could find you have a hobby for life!

So go on. What's stopping you? Get out there. Be imaginative, be creative but – above all – have fun!

Jeremy Beadle

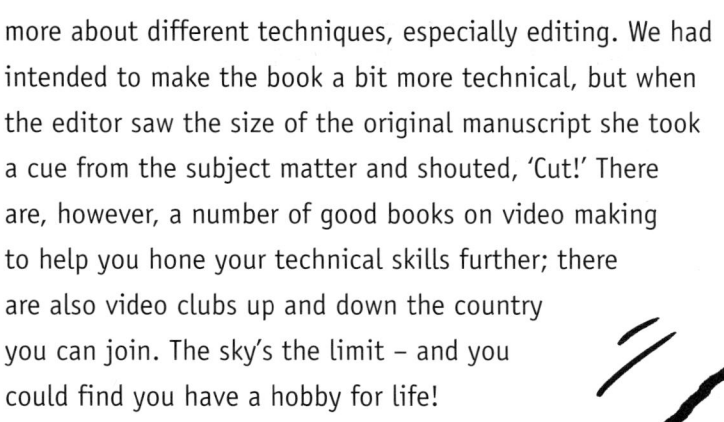

Beadle's Ten Commandments for Better Comedy Videos

★ Keep it short
★ Keep it simple
★ Keep it funny
★ Think visually; people watch more than they listen
★ Having a good idea is more important than having expensive equipment
★ Put yourself in the audience's place – would you enjoy it?
★ Improvise rather than spend
★ Use a tripod
★ Be nice to your cast and crew
★ Have fun!

Ideas for Your Blockbuster?

The real work was thinking, just thinking . . .
Charlie Chaplin

Every Blockbuster starts with an *idea*. So the very first step is to have an idea. Easier said than done, right? No one really knows where ideas come from. It's probably something to do with interaction between different parts of the human brain. You see or hear something. Your brain associates it with something else and – bingo – you have an idea. It may be the inspiration for the world's best Blockbuster – or you might just decide it's time for lunch.

Trying Too Hard

Finding just the right idea for your Blockbuster is perhaps the most difficult part of the entire process. Remember that ideas aren't dogs. They don't always come when you call. Trying too hard to come up with a brilliant idea can give your brain the equivalent of 'stage fright'. It'll seize up and refuse to go on. Try to relax instead. Don't impose a strict deadline on yourself. Don't tell your brain, 'Give me a good idea by six o'clock or I'll force you to listen to old Osmonds albums – and you know how that hurts!'

Politely tell your brain you want an idea for a Blockbuster and then go about your normal business. Periodically, your brain should chirp in with an idea: 'How about this one, master?' If it's an idea with legs (don't try to imagine an idea with legs, we're talking metaphorically), your brain will then start to expand on it all by itself. You'll find that, much to your delight, not only has your brain furnished you with an idea – but it's now racing away writing the script for you as well!

Applying the 24-Hour Test

Unfortunately, the brain can sometimes come up with bad ideas as well as good ones. It's not always easy to tell them apart. Bad ideas start wars, fill your house with furniture you later detest or end up as ITV sit-coms.

Sleep on your idea. If it still feels like a good idea the next day, then it probably is.

Your Starters for Ten

Throughout this whole section of the book, I'll be providing as many raw ideas as I can for your Blockbusters. I'm not going to write the scripts for you (you couldn't afford me), but you can take any of these ideas quite freely as your starting point and develop them yourself. That way, they're uniquely yours.

Some Useful Sources for Ideas

Your life's a joke

Some of the very best ideas for Blockbusters will come out of things you've seen or that may have happened to you. A whole sketch might just play out in front of you, or you may overhear someone say a simple sentence which sparks an idea off in your head.

Keep a notebook – and take it everywhere you go. Even take it to bed. Take it to the bathroom with you because – and I guarantee this – ideas come at the oddest times and places. If you don't write them down there and then, twenty minutes later they're gone forever.

Newspapers

Bob Monkhouse can do a half-hour routine out of one single newspaper. All right, so it's a 1952 newspaper, but so what? The material is all there, delivered to your door every day. As you read your paper, keep an eye out for stories that strike you as odd, or funny, or ironic. Think about turning them on their heads or twisting them around in some way. There's bound to be something in there which would make a great Blockbuster.

Beadle Tips

YOU KNOW IT'S A BAD IDEA WHEN:

★ IT RELIES ON A FRIEND BEING ABLE TO LEND YOU AN ARMOURED CAR

★ IT HAS THE WORD 'INFERNO' IN THE TITLE

★ IT INVOLVES YOUR GRANNY IN A TOPLESS SCENE

★ IT HAS TO BE FILMED IN LIMA

★ THE WHOLE PIECE DEPENDS ON STRAPPING A CAMCORDER TO A PUMA

★ THE SCRIPT WEIGHS MORE THAN YOU DO

★ IT'S BASED ON A SLAVIC PUN (THAT YOU CAN'T QUITE REMEMBER PROPERLY)

★ YOUR SCRIPT CALLS FOR A 20-MINUTE STOP-FRAME ANIMATION SEQUENCE INVOLVING TWO ROOT VEGETABLES

★ IT RELIES ON CAMEO APPEARANCES BY ARNOLD SCHWARZENEGGER AND THE QUEEN MUM (WHO APPEAR IN THE SAME SCENE WITH MACHETES)

Music to the eyes

Think about bringing a song to life. If there ever was a song waiting to be turned into a Blockbuster, for example, it's the Rolling Stones' '(I Can't Get No) Satisfaction'. It's a gift for a series of sight gags about the frustrations of everyday life – the post office closing just as you arrive, a hideously long queue for the loo, a pretty girl turning you down and so on.

Song titles will spark off ideas. How about 'Wild Thing' or 'I Can't Help Myself'? 'They're Coming to Take Me Away, Ha Ha!' or 'Help The Aged'? Go to your record collection and just read the titles.

Alternatively, you could do a 'tribute' to one group and use an assortment of their songs in a medley. Let's say, for example, you choose The Beatles. You've got a baby who's just starting to toddle. Imagine the charming scenes you can capture on video with the Beatles' accompaniment – 'Help' and 'I Wanna Hold Your Hand' as you capture her trying to walk; 'Get Back' for when she wanders off somewhere; 'She Loves You', 'Love Me Do' and 'And I Love Her' for quiet cuddles; 'Yellow Submarine' in the bath and 'Paperback Writer' as she crayons. There's 'Hello Goodbye' for those cute little waves and 'I'm Only Sleeping' or 'A Hard Day's Night' for cot scenes. Trust me, you can even use 'Strawberry Fields Forever' (just put a plate of strawberries in front of a baby and see what happens!). OK. So 'Sgt. Pepper's Lonely Hearts Club Band' might cause a few problems – just ignore that one, all right!

There aren't many groups as rich in songs as The Beatles, so you might like to string several songs on one theme together from different acts instead. The effect is the same. You can produce 'tributes' to babies, dogs, kissing, schooldays, Christmas, flatulence, laziness, romance, driving, bad behaviour, rain, your home, me – you name it.

The *Guinness Book of Hit Singles* is an ideal source for song titles.

KID'S COMICS AND COMIC STRIPS

WHILE YOU'VE GOT THE NEWSPAPER, TURN TO THE COMIC STRIPS. STRIPS LIKE ANDY CAPP AND FRED BASSETT ARE ESSENTIALLY STORYBOARDS (SEE P.58-59) WAITING FOR YOU TO TURN THEM INTO LITTLE BLOCKBUSTERS. YOU'VE GOT A DOG? GREAT – WHY NOT BRING THAT FRED BASSETT STRIP TO LIFE? YOU HAVEN'T GOT A DOG BUT YOU'VE GOT A COMFY SOFA TO SPRAWL ON? FINE. YOU'RE ALL SET TO DO ANDY CAPP. KID'S COMICS, LIKE THE *BEANO* AND *DANDY*, CONTAIN LONGER COMIC STRIPS. THEY'RE MORE ADVANCED STORYBOARDS, CONTAINING A SERIES OF JOKES AND A PUNCHLINE. YOU CAN ADAPT THEM IN JUST THE SAME WAY.

The Mix 'n' Match Ideas Generator

Your brain works by mixing and matching different ideas, so why not deliberately give it two very different ideas and see what amalgamation it produces?

For example, you can have a lot of fun by mixing together two very different TV shows or films. Try it. Take one title from column A and then one title from column B so, for example, you end up with *Planet of the Apes* meets *The Sound of Music*. Now try to imagine what the weird amalgamation would be like if you saw it on TV or the big screen. Let your imagination really run wild! If it tickles your funny bone, then there's your sketch idea!

Ideas Generator

Column A

PLANET OF THE APES

JAWS

THE TERMINATOR

TRUE GRIT

STAR WARS

THE DIRTY DOZEN

CONAN THE BARBARIAN

GODZILLA

TARZAN

INVASION OF THE BODY SNATCHERS

DELIVERANCE

TORA! TORA! TORA!

JURASSIC PARK

DIRTY HARRY

THE EXORCIST

MAD MAX BEYOND THUNDERDOME

Column B

THE SOUND OF MUSIC

THE BRADY BUNCH

THE TELETUBBIES

LA CAGE AUX FOLLES

THE FULL MONTY

WISH YOU WERE HERE?

GRANGE HILL

LASSIE

OLIVER!

THE 10 O'CLOCK NEWS

LAST OF THE SUMMER WINE

ANIMAL HOSPITAL

SOME MOTHERS DO 'AVE 'EM

THE SOOTY SHOW

SESAME STREET

MARY POPPINS

Useful Comedy Techniques

Good comedy may look totally anarchic and ferociously creative, but there are age-old, tried and tested comedy formulae behind it all. When you know what they are, these formulae act like comedy blueprints from which you can build your sketch. Let's look at a few now . . .

Shocking Comedy Sketches!

Scholars through the ages have worked tirelessly to explain the humble joke. Whole books have been written about the psychology of humour. What it all boils down to is that people laugh when the unexpected happens, when they're shocked or surprised. This doesn't mean shocked in an offended or grossly indecent way. When you get arrested for videoing that staggeringly obscene sketch in the high street, please don't go telling the police Jeremy Beadle told you to do it. I did not.

Surprise, Surprise

One of the essential elements of comedy is surprising the audience. Ambush them. Get them to expect one thing – and then deliver something else entirely. Here's one of the oldest examples in the book (and when I say 'old' I mean primeval...).

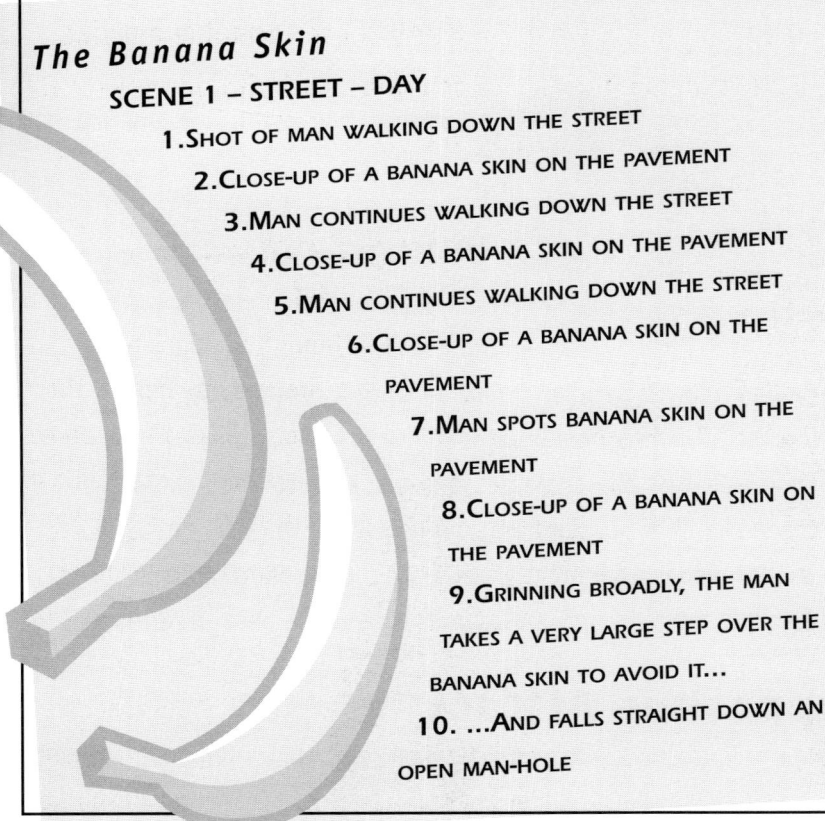

The Banana Skin
SCENE 1 – STREET – DAY
1. SHOT OF MAN WALKING DOWN THE STREET
2. CLOSE-UP OF A BANANA SKIN ON THE PAVEMENT
3. MAN CONTINUES WALKING DOWN THE STREET
4. CLOSE-UP OF A BANANA SKIN ON THE PAVEMENT
5. MAN CONTINUES WALKING DOWN THE STREET
6. CLOSE-UP OF A BANANA SKIN ON THE PAVEMENT
7. MAN SPOTS BANANA SKIN ON THE PAVEMENT
8. CLOSE-UP OF A BANANA SKIN ON THE PAVEMENT
9. GRINNING BROADLY, THE MAN TAKES A VERY LARGE STEP OVER THE BANANA SKIN TO AVOID IT...
10. ...AND FALLS STRAIGHT DOWN AN OPEN MAN-HOLE

Come on Down!

One sure way to get laughs is by taking something grand and then mixing it with the everyday.

On a simple level, this is the policeman slipping on a banana skin. Charlie Chaplin knew that you get a much bigger laugh seeing a policeman slip over than you would a street urchin. We love seeing figures of authority or people with great dignity brought down a notch or two. Remember that, when you choose a 'victim' for your humour.

However, you can do much more with this idea. Take the example on the top of the next page.

THE RUNNING JOKE

INTRODUCING A JOKE EARLY ON AND REVISITING IT CAN BE USED TO GET LAUGHS. FOR EXAMPLE, YOU MIGHT INTRODUCE A CHARACTER WHO HAS A NERVOUS TIC THAT MAKES HIM LOOK AS IF HE'S WINKING WHEN HE ISN'T. THIS COULD CROP UP AT INOPPORTUNE MOMENTS IN YOUR VIDEO, LIKE WHEN HE'S TALKING TO A GIRL (WHO THINKS HE'S MAKING AN IMPROPER SUGGESTION), A MAN (DITTO), A POLICEMAN (WHO THINKS HE'S OFFERING A BRIBE) OR EVEN SOMEONE ELSE WITH A REAL NERVOUS TIC – WHO THINKS HE'S TAKING THE MICKEY. ANOTHER RUNNING JOKE MIGHT BE TO HAVE SOMEONE WHOSE MOBILE PHONE GOES OFF AT EMBARRASSING MOMENTS – LIKE WHEN HE'S SEDUCING A GIRL, IN A CONFESSION BOOTH, AT A FUNERAL ETC.

OF COURSE, THE RUNNING JOKE COULD ALSO BE USED TO ADD HUMOUR TO A SCENE WHERE THE JOKE IS PURELY INCIDENTAL – FOR INSTANCE, HAVING A CHARACTER WHO SLEEPWALKS THROUGH VARIOUS SCENES, AVOIDING DANGER BY THE SLIGHTEST WHISKER. IN A CASE LIKE THIS, YOU SHOULD AIM TO HAVE A CONCLUSION TO THE RUNNING JOKE – MAYBE AT THE END OF YOUR VIDEO SOMEONE WAKES HIM UP AND IT'S THE SHOCK THAT FINALLY KILLS HIM.

Weather lovely.
Wish you were here.
Love Darth x x x

Inject the everyday into the grand and
pompous. Lord Darth Vader on holiday.
(Photo courtesy of the Skegness
Tourist Authority)

Star Bores

Think of Darth Vader – the Dark Lord
of the Sith himself. A grand figure.
Now ask yourself:

★Where does he go on holiday?

★How does he go to the toilet?

★What's he like when he's not
at work?

★What if he lost his job and had
to sign on?

★Indeed, what would he be like
at a job interview?

★Imagine him walking the dog
or visiting the chip shop or having a bath.

★He was married at some point, so what was Mrs Vader like?

★Did they live in a nice little semi?

And that's just one character, and one example. You could get
a dozen sketch ideas from that alone. All you need for the costume
is a Darth Vader mask from a novelty or comic shop, a black sheet
for a cape and a pair of wellie boots and you're off and running!

Opposites Attract

People who behave differently from the way they should will surprise
and usually delight an audience.

Remember 'Hell's Grannies' – the delinquent OAPs who beat up
innocent Hells Angels in *Monty Python's Flying Circus*?

How do you do this? Let's take nuns, for example. They're always
quiet and pious – but what if they weren't? What's the last thing
you'd associate with a nun? Tag team wrestling? Indiana Jones-type
adventures? Rugby League? Showdowns with six guns at High Noon
on Main Street? *'Fill your hand, Sister Assumpta...'*

Turn it around for a minute. Now think of the SAS – butch lads one
and all. What's the last thing you associate with them? Flower
arranging? Bitching over boyfriends? Crying over a tearjerker movie
in the mess hall? Make-up tips?

Put two opposite extremes together and you can usually come up with a very amusing little sketch.

Cruelty

We know we shouldn't but we love laughing at others' misfortunes, whether it's as basic as seeing someone get hit in the face with a custard pie, or the savouring of the moment when the 'victim' discovers, for example, that their car – their beloved pride and joy – has been towed away to the car crusher by mistake.

Why do we take pleasure in laughing at someone else in this heartless way? Well, apart from enjoying the comic spectacle, while we're laughing at our victim we're relieved it isn't happening to us. (Look out the window to see if your car's still there . . .)

Build-up

What makes a really good laugh is the build-up to the comedy climax. It's the satisfaction that we know what's about to happen before the victim does. For example, we know that the man's boss, who he's cruelly mimicking, is sitting right behind him, or that the woman he's chatting up at a bar is actually a drag artiste.

The longer you can draw out this comic suspense, the funnier the joke often is.

Misunderstanding

Like mistaken identity, humour can come from putting your characters in a situation where they think they should be doing A, whereas in reality they should be doing B – for example, the builder who demolishes house 19 when he should be at number 61, or the gangster's wife who mixes up the black plastic bin liner containing the used notes from the bank robbery with the black plastic bin liner containing garden waste – and it's dustbin day.

Absurdity

The wilder the idea, the funnier it usually is. See over the page for a few bizarre comic premises:

MISTAKEN IDENTITY

A COMMON SOURCE OF COMEDY IS TO PLACE A CHARACTER OR CHARACTERS IN A SITUATION WHERE THEY'RE CLEARLY OUT OF THEIR DEPTH – AND TOO FAR IN EVER TO EXTRACT THEMSELVES, EITHER BECAUSE OF PRIDE, EMBARRASSMENT, SHAME OR FEAR (OR MAYBE THEY DON'T EVEN REALISE THEIR ERROR). PLACE YOUR CHARACTERS WHERE THERE IS A REAL CONTRAST BETWEEN THEIR PRIVATE, MUNDANE LIVES AND THE SITUATION THEY FIND THEMSELVES IN. HAVING AN ORDINARY DOCTOR MISTAKEN FOR THE WORLD'S LEADING BRAIN TRANSPLANT SURGEON IS NOT THAT FUNNY, BUT WHAT IF A TV REPAIRMAN IS IN THAT PREDICAMENT?

The crew of a U-boat are tense. There is the danger of depth-charge attack and they're practising 'silent routine'. Just then the captain admits that he's terrified of confined spaces. To stop him going mad the crew have to try and convince him that the U-boat is larger than it is. Much, much larger. Then the radio operator gets scared. He can't stand wide-open spaces – that's why he joined the U-boats in the first place . . .

Sherlock Holmes is assisted by Dr Watson. They're at the scene of a crime looking for clues. These are all around them – footprints, fingerprints, even a signed confession pinned to a wall. The trouble is that Holmes can't see them – he's found far, far less obvious things like minute fibres from a suit, ash from a cigarette etc. All the time Watson tries to point out what he's missing, Holmes just pooh-poohs his suggestions . . .

Police chasing a getaway car run out of petrol. The crooks think they're home and dry but, in their excitement, manage to stall their car. They can't start it as they have a flat battery. The chase continues with both the police and the crooks pushing their cars – firing guns at each other as the chase continues at 4mph. They reach a garage and pull up alongside each other, still shooting – while the police fill up with petrol and the crooks get a jump start . . .

Bizarre situations? Yes. Impossible? Maybe. A source of humour? Certainly. All you need is your imagination.

Incongruous Situations

Similar to the above is taking a character and putting him/her/it in a situation where they'd never, ever end up. How about a surgeon in an operating theatre who can't stand the sight of blood; a taxi driver who admits to his passenger that he doesn't know how to drive (and the passenger has to teach him); a veteran drill sergeant in charge of a pack of cub scouts;

a porcupine at an interview for a job at a balloon factory (best of luck with the costume for that one!)?

You know these people (and porcupines) wouldn't end up where they are, but that's precisely what makes the situations funny and ripe for exploiting.

Escalation

Take a comic event and expand it to the point of absurdity. For example, a waiter accidentally knocks a glass of wine over a diner. The diner mops his lap and then takes his partner's wine and splashes the waiter. Not one to let this lie, the waiter dips his fingers in the soup and flicks the diner in the face with it. The diner retaliates by getting a handful of spaghetti and throwing this at the waiter, who then proceeds to empty a bowl of parmesan cheese over the diner's head. When the food runs out on the table, other customers' food is appropriated – along with the entire dessert trolley.

The whole sequence is carried out with sophistication and decorum and escalates to the point when both the waiter and the diner are covered head to toe in food. The last bowl of food in the entire restaurant ends up over the waiter and the diner looks triumphant. Top that! Then the waiter presents him with the bill . . .

Comedy Props

Whether it's someone getting their foot caught in one of those electric shoe-cleaning devices found in hotels or dealing with a malfunctioning robot, you can always rely on props to get laughs. The silent comedians built their careers on them. So too has Mr Bean.

The trick is to write a series of prop gags that happen in the same place (this could be one sequence in a comedy video or the basis of the whole video itself).

Take a gymnasium – a place that's filled with the sort of props that lend themselves to a range of simple gags, all easily filmed in one location.

3 Prop Gags Set in a Gymnasium

WE START WITH OUR CHARACTER PUTTING HIS CLOTHES IN A LOCKER. HE PUTS HIS SHIRT AND TROUSERS IN, BUT WHEN HE RE-OPENS IT TO ADD HIS SHOES, HIS CLOTHES HAVE GONE. THEY'VE SOMEHOW MOVED TO A DIFFERENT LOCKER!

OUR CHARACTER NOW ENTERS THE GYM ITSELF, WEARING A WALKMAN. WE CAN HEAR (MUFFLED) WHAT HE'S LISTENING TO AND HE GETS ON AN EXERCISE BIKE. AS HE PEDALS FASTER THE MUSIC SPEEDS UP. AS HE SLOWS DOWN IT SLURS. HE JUST CAN'T FIGURE OUT WHY.

HE PICKS UP A PAIR OF (DOCTORED) CHEST EXPANDERS. HE PULLS THEM ACROSS HIS CHEST BUT THEY REMAIN EXPANDED – HE'S STRETCHED THEM TOO FAR.

Slapstick and the Art of Custard Pie Throwing

You don't have to dress up as a clown or silent-movie star for a custard pie routine (although you could). What would be funnier is to take custard pie throwing into an incongruous situation, for instance, a funeral wake, a board meeting, a heart transplant operation, a meeting of the United Nations Security Council, a TV debate between politicians etc. In these cases the humour derives from the absurdity of the scenario (e.g. UN members throwing custard pies) as well as the mess made by the pies themselves.

Custard pies, banana skins, dangling off clock hands, getting hit by planks of wood, narrowly avoiding a large pane of glass being shifted by two weary labourers – do I need to say any more? Actually, the editor says I do – I've got 144 pages to fill. We all know what slapstick is, but very few of us know how to do it. Its success depends on grace, understatement and, above all, impeccable comic timing (not to mention adequate health insurance).

Even something as seemingly simple as throwing a custard pie is a true art.

Don't laugh. Custard pie throwing *is* an art – one that goes back eighty-five years, when Mabel Normand threw the very first pie on film in 1913, while working at Mack Sennett's Keystone Studios.

However, most of the laughs derived from custard pie throwing don't come from the act itself. They come from the *expectation* of what's going to happen. The longer you can keep up this expectation, then the funnier the reaction will be.

This can be expressed by the following formula:

where H = humour

CP = custard pie

D = distance

V = velocity

T^2 = time pie is held before being thrown

$$H = \frac{(CP \times D) \times T^2}{V}$$

This is known as the Pie-Thagoras theorem (sorry!).

To throw or to shove?

To be thrown any reasonable distance, a pie needs to have considerable weight. The trouble is that heavy pies/plates are dangerous and, whereas most actors hit by pies don't mind losing their dignity, they *do* mind losing their teeth. That's why most pies are *shoved* in their victim's face. Not only is this more accurate, but it enables the pies to be lighter and made much more simply:

Ingredients

Q: When is a custard pie not a custard pie? A: When it's a paper plate covered in either whipped cream or shaving foam. This method makes them lightweight and they won't knock you out.

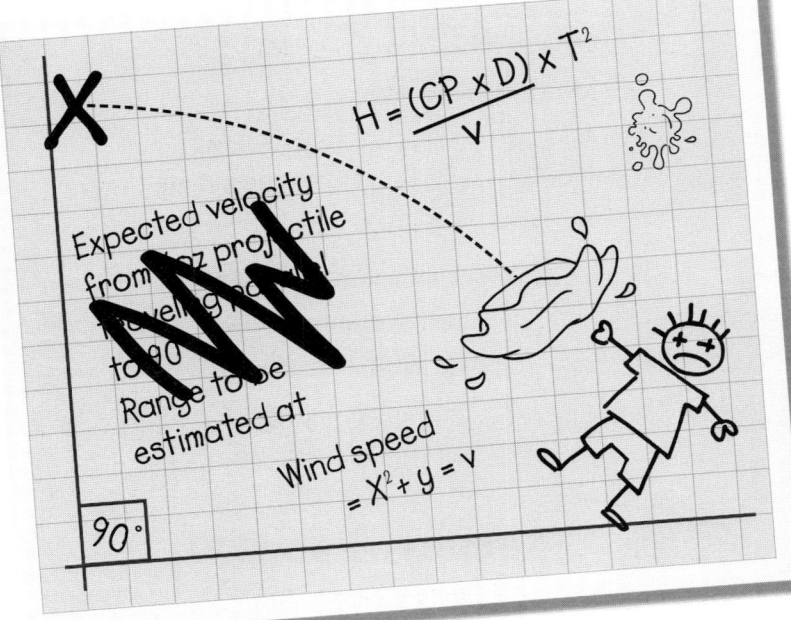

$$H = \frac{(CP \times D)}{V} \times T^2$$

Expected velocity from 6oz projectile travelling at ...
to go ...
Range to be estimated at

Wind speed $= X^2 + y = V$

90°

Beadle Tips

HITTING SOMEONE WITH A PIE ISN'T ENOUGH; TRY AND BUILD IN SOME ADDITIONAL GAGS. FOR EXAMPLE:

★ YOU'RE CONSTANTLY INTERRUPTED BY SOMEONE COMING INTO THE ROOM

★ YOU KEEP MISSING YOUR TARGET

★ YOU GET HIT BY A CONCEALED PIE HELD BY YOUR VICTIM

★ YOU SHOVE THE PIE BUT YOUR VICTIM DUCKS AND IT HITS SOMEONE ELSE

★ THE AUDIENCE THINKS YOU'RE GOING TO SHOVE THE PIE IN YOUR VICTIM'S FACE BUT YOU PUT IT ON THEIR CHAIR INSTEAD

★ YOU PUT THE PIE DOWN SOMEWHERE AND FORGET ABOUT IT – ONLY TO SIT IN IT YOURSELF

The delivery

For the best effect you need to conceal the pie from your victim, but keep it within sight of the viewers so they know what to expect. I can't stress enough the need to exploit the anticipation of the audience before you throw it. Look at your victim, then at the pie, smile, look back to your victim again, then back at your pie, smile again . . .

BE CAREFUL WHEN MAKING CUSTARD PIES OUT OF SHAVING FOAMS CONTAINING MENTHOL, AS THIS CAN IRRITATE THE EYES.

17

Creating Comedy Characters

Sometimes, it's easier to think of an idea if you have a character in mind first. Comedy is filled with stock characters for you to use if you want to. Think how many comedy sketches you've seen featuring these staple, modern-day characters:

DRUNKS

DOOR-TO-DOOR SALESMEN

VICARS

LECHERS

HUSBANDS AND WIVES

DOCTORS

SHOPKEEPERS

JUDGES AND LAWYERS

PILOTS

REPORTERS

SOCCER PLAYERS

TV INTERVIEWERS

SECRETARIES

MOTHERS-IN-LAW

MPs

POLICE

SHORT-SIGHTED PEOPLE

TRAFFIC WARDENS

CHEFS

ZOO KEEPERS

SPIES

PUB LANDLORDS

WAITERS

TV PRESENTERS

You can probably think of many others. Don't be ashamed to use them. They're ready-made characters for you, available off the shelf, and your audience will immediately recognise and understand them.

Famous People

So you're no Faith Brown, Bobby Davro or Rory Bremner? So what? You can buy novelty masks of famous people from joke and fancy dress shops. Then the sky's the limit. You want to film 'Frankenstein Meets Prince Charles'? No problem. You want Ronald Reagan to appear on your *Mastermind* sketch? Sorted. You want to feature Lady Thatcher in your remake of *Basic Instinct*? Not a problem (at least not a technical one – a psychological one, perhaps . . .).

Creating Your Own Comedy Characters

Curse that Harry Enfield for being so talented. Think of all the classic comedy characters he's created over the years, from Stavros to Smashey and Nicey to The Self-Righteous Brothers and Tim Nice-But-Dim. How does he do it? In a word – observation. These are real people he's met, blown up, and exaggerated out of all proportion, rather like a cartoonist does when he draws a caricature of someone.

Doing this is a definite skill – and hard work too. Look at the most interesting and unusual people you know. Ask yourself what makes them that way. Then take all those outrageous elements, throw away any trace of any normal characteristics and you should be left with a usable comedy caricature.

Zany Characters

Creating 'zany', off-the-wall characters is a different skill. It's more about imagination and less about people-watching. These kinds of characters are usually created – just like comedy ideas – by crashing two wildly different concepts together and looking at what results.

Let's meet a few . . .

Mr Medieval – taking nostalgia just a bit too far?

Mr Medieval

For some reason Mr Medieval thinks he's still in the dark ages, despite having a perfectly normal twentieth-century family. The electric light bulb is diabolical wizardry, planes coming in near his home in Hounslow are fiery dragons and he throws his bodily waste out of the window too – much to the horror of his neighbours . . .

By day he plies his trade by pulling a hand cart past the neat semis, commanding 'Bring out your dead.' Business is not good.

The local mayor is baffled by offers of tithes from his vegetable garden, the constabulary are alarmed by his archery practice on the common and the local travel agents are trying to stop him coming in to book up for 'a crusade to the holy land to drive out the heathen Infidels'.

Mr Medieval is typical of what is called a 'fish out of water' character. He's someone who doesn't belong where he is, like Rambo at a church coffee morning or Dale Winton on an SAS raid.

OTHER 'FISH OUT OF WATER' CHARACTERS YOU MIGHT LIKE TO CONSIDER INCLUDE:
★ JOHNNY NAPALM – THE VIETNAM VETERAN WHO LIVES IN THE LARDER
★ TARZAN'S AUNTIE
★ THE EMPEROR OF AMERSHAM
★ DRACULA'S BEST MATE DAVE
★ DR NEANDERTHAL, MD
★ MY HUSBAND, THE ALIEN BLOB

The door-to-door aircraft carrier salesman

Yes – he's a salesman who sells aircraft carriers door-to-door. He hasn't sold one yet, but when he does, his salesman's commission will see him on Easy Street for the rest of his life.

Imagine his desperate sales patter, trying to convince housewives that what's missing from their lives is an aircraft carrier. Imagine his swerving and dodging to avoid questions like 'How much does it cost?' or 'Where could I put it?' Instead, he'll concentrate on the positive aspects and special offers like 'It comes free with 1500 sailors' and 'Buy now and we'll throw in a Squadron of F-14 Tomcats at half price!' or 'There's never been a better time to buy a carrier of your very own!'

The door-to-door aircraft carrier salesman is the very opposite of Mr Medieval. He's sane for one thing. It's his crazy job he's trying to deal with as best he can, but we've still crashed two very different ideas together to produce him.

Now let's simply reverse that. Take a sensible job, and give it to unlikely people to perform and you get:

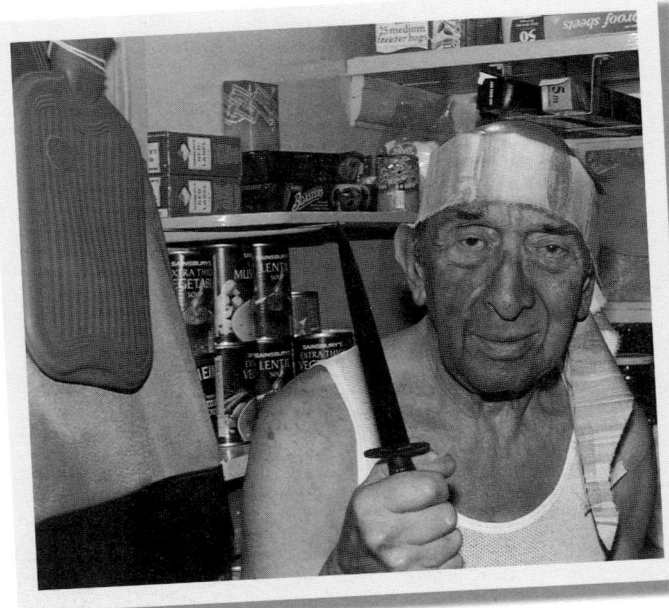

Comedy characters: how about inventing someone like Johnny Napalm, the Vietnam veteran who lives in the larder?

Caveman Cops

Caveman Cops are the world's first police officers, using all the clichés of tough American police officers – 'I know what you're thinking punk; Did I fire one arrow from this bow or two?' – to do a dirty job in an even dirtier world of fire smuggling, joy riders on mammoths and vicious Neanderthals with a psychopathic hatred of Homo Sapiens, where death is only an ass's jawbone away.

OTHER EXAMPLES WHERE TWO COMPLETELY DIFFERENT IDEAS ARE COMBINED MIGHT INCLUDE:

★ FARMER GILES AND HIS FURNITURE FARM
★ BARRY STOTT – GRIM REAPER
★ DEADSHOT DONOVAN – HUNTING BIG CHEESES ON THE SERENGETI
★ MAGNUS, FRIDGE WRESTLER
★ DAVY JONES AND HIS RENT-A-WALL ENTERPRISE
★ TINA TOPPS – BUILDING BEAUTICIAN

OTHER CHARACTERS MIGHT INCLUDE:
★ MY RED INDIAN HEADMASTER
★ FRANKENSTEIN'S BISTRO
★ CALIGULA'S COMEDY CLINIC
★ THE MENSA TUMBLERS
★ GARDENER'S WORLD WITH GENERAL PATTON

SCRATCH TAPES

HOW DO YOU FEEL ABOUT INTERVIEWING WILLIAM HAGUE OR TONY BLAIR? YOU CAN, WITH THE MAGIC OF VIDEO! YOU SIMPLY RECORD AN INTERVIEW OFF THE TV. (ALL RIGHT, ALL RIGHT, I KNOW IT'S COPYRIGHT AND YOU'LL PROBABLY GO TO HELL FOR DOING IT – BUT IT'S FUN.) YOU THEN VIDEO YOURSELF AS THE INTERVIEWER AND ASK YOUR OWN QUESTIONS. LATER, YOU EDIT IN WILLIAM OR TONY'S REPLIES (SEE P.130) SO THAT IT APPEARS THEY'RE ANSWERING YOU . . .

So you're almost completely useless?

You

Yes, I think that's fair to say and I know that my party are behind me one hundred per cent in this

WILLIAM HAGUE

Characters with a Quirk

Sometimes, all you need to create a fresh comedy character is to give him or her one little obsessive quirk, vice or trait which defines him. Let's meet a few:

Mr Windy

The disturbingly Frank Spencer-like Barry Blake has a problem – a chronic flatulence problem to be precise. And it's getting worse. And louder. And more odiferous. How he ever got to become Foreign Secretary is a total mystery . . .

Brian Brett – TV vet

Brian is a TV vet with an unusual attitude – he hates pets. This is essentially a 'to camera' piece with him answering questions 'live' on a portable telephone from viewers phoning in. His philosophy is 'have fun with your pet'. This is not necessarily in the pet's best interests . . .

Creating a fresh new comedy character is a very real achievement. If you do it, give yourself a pat on the back. He belongs to you 100 per cent – and you might even like to consider using him as a running character in several different Blockbusters!

Quentin Diablo, he solves baffling mysteries ... and does a great perm at his salon...

OTHERS MIGHT INCLUDE:

★ A HUSBAND AND WIFE WHO SPEAK TO EACH OTHER ENTIRELY IN SUN HEADLINES

★ MR ROGET'S THESAURUS

★ A MAN WHO SHOUTS EVERY SENTENCE

★ A DOCTOR WHOSE SPEECH IS AS BAD AS HIS WRITING

★ SOMEONE WHO'S UNBEARABLY PERKY AND CHEERFUL, NO MATTER HOW TERRIBLE THINGS GET . . .

★ A RICH UNCLE WHO'S CONSTANTLY GIVING BIGGER AND BIGGER GIFTS TO HIS NEPHEWS

★ MR LITERAL (HE INTERPRETS EVERYTHING LITERALLY)

★ MR DON'T LET ANYONE GET A WORD IN EDGEWAYS . . .

★ A PSYCHIATRIST WHO READS MEANING INTO EVERYTHING

★ MR TOO NICE

★ BILLY JONES WHO HAS FALLEN MADLY, PASSIONATELY, DEEPLY, SENSUOUSLY IN LOVE – WITH THE M4 MOTORWAY

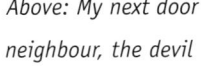
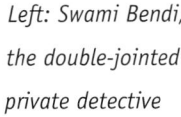

Above: My next door neighbour, the devil

Left: Swami Bendi, the double-jointed private detective

The Art of Parody

Parodies are by far the most popular form of Blockbusters to make. You can parody almost anything you see on TV or at the cinema. Here are just a few examples of genres (that's posh media talk for 'subjects') you might like to consider.

Great Movie Clichés

Why not re-create one of those classic moments of cinema, and then give it your own unique twist? Some scenes you might like to consider include:

★The final airport scene in *Casablanca*

★King Kong atop the Empire State Building

★The tossed bone that becomes a spaceship in *2001: A Space Odyssey*

★The shower scene in *Psycho*

★Burt Lancaster and Deborah Kerr on the beach in *From Here to Eternity*

★The Allied POWs whistling 'Colonel Bogey' in *Bridge on the River Kwai*

Quiz Shows

You've got to go all out to parody a quiz show or a game show – because most of them seem to parody themselves these days!

Still, it's a fun thing to do and easily recognisable to your audience. You need an extra-cheesy over-the-top host, capable of both fawning and insulting, a gaggle of very bad jokes and a stupid idea for a quiz show. Imagine these for example:

Drink Yourself Rich!!

Painful Sitting Positions!

You Bet Your Dog!

FROG OF FORTUNE!

YOUR MONEY OR YOUR LIFE!

Swear Words!

Win that Cheese!

A Great Pair of Hits!

Family Shouting!

Bite Your Host!

A Question of Estate Agency!

Win, Lose or Go Nub-nub-nub-nub-nub!

WHOSE SOCKS?

With Des Lennis
Tonight at Eight

'Whose Socks?' – the fantastic new prime-time quiz show (though some people think it stinks)

BOTTOMS UP!
(Don't ask...)

Knock Out!
(The great new quiz show that combines general knowledge with professional boxing! Hey, if Jim Davidson can do it with snooker...)

Once you know what your quiz show is about, the sketch will virtually write itself. Don't forget, all quiz shows build to a climax – a sudden-death play off or all-or-nothing end game, often against the clock. That's where your punchline lies.

Kids love performing in a DIY pop video. (Even the Spice Girls had to start somewhere.)

Pop Videos

Can you write, sing and play an original song? You can? Well, you're too talented by half, so go off and make your video now. You star.

If you can't – and you want to use someone else's song on your video – chances are that it's copyright and, legally speaking, you shouldn't copy it on to your tape. You are taking the bread out of Mick Jagger's mouth when you do this. However, Mick Jagger is very thin, so this must be a very common practice.

Now, do you choose a favourite song – or one you particularly hate? That's up to you. You can also choose whether to parody a particular video you've seen or create a totally new one, sending up the performer. When Hale & Pace 'did' Michael Bolton, for example, they concentrated on his permed hair and prominent nose. When Dawn French 'did' Bjork, she concentrated on the fact that Bjork's 'eccentric'. Whatever you choose, you'll probably need a real *Stars in Their Eyes* treatment to look halfway like who you're parodying. It's worth spending a slab of your budget on make-up and costume to achieve this.

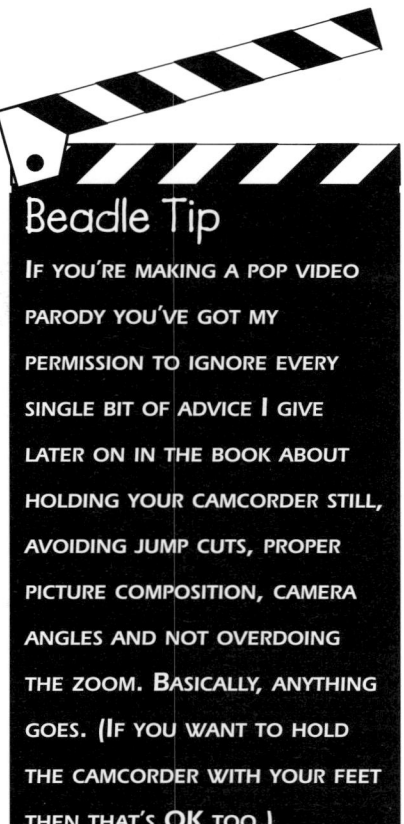

Beadle Tip

IF YOU'RE MAKING A POP VIDEO PARODY YOU'VE GOT MY PERMISSION TO IGNORE EVERY SINGLE BIT OF ADVICE I GIVE LATER ON IN THE BOOK ABOUT HOLDING YOUR CAMCORDER STILL, AVOIDING JUMP CUTS, PROPER PICTURE COMPOSITION, CAMERA ANGLES AND NOT OVERDOING THE ZOOM. BASICALLY, ANYTHING GOES. (IF YOU WANT TO HOLD THE CAMCORDER WITH YOUR FEET THEN THAT'S OK TOO.)

Historical Drama

Historical Dramas are fab! You have all of history to choose from. You can go painting with Van Gogh, bring down the ten commandments with Moses, walk the wards of Scutari with Florence Nightingale or steal from the rich to give to the poor with Robin Hood.

Suffragettes, warrior lords, prophets, kings, adventurers, saints, Greek philosophers – they're all ripe to have the mickey taken out of them by you. Imagine doing a piece about Plato, Socrates, Aristotle and Archimedes – in the style of The Monkees ('Hey, hey, we're the philosophers!').

Another idea is to play a 'What If' game. What if they had television back then? Imagine the 'Attila the Hun chat show' or the caveman version of *Mr & Mrs*. Would the medieval equivalent of Claire Rayner be doling out advice on avoiding the Black Death?

Low Budget Blockbusters

How about trying to re-create the film of your choice – in sixty seconds and with next to no budget? Be ambitious. Do *Jurassic Park* or *Gone With The Wind*. Do *Ben Hur* and *The Greatest Story Ever Told* – or *The Longest Day* or *Star Wars*. Trying to tell the story so quickly with what you have to hand will almost guarantee an hilarious Blockbuster. (I used to do this on one of my radio shows as '60 Second Masterpieces'; these led on to *Beadle's Hot Shots* on TV.)

Westerns

Westerns have been parodied – a lot. Just because it has been done before doesn't mean you shouldn't do it, but try to be original in this area.

Think about the Indians. Is there a big fight over the best names? Do the losers get lumbered with Running Sore or Yellow Skunk?

And then there's the cowboys. How do you become a 'Six Gun for Hire'? And where do you hire one? Is there a version of the Reed Employment Agency for Temp Gunslingers?

If you use your imagination, there's still a lot you can do that's new and fresh . . .

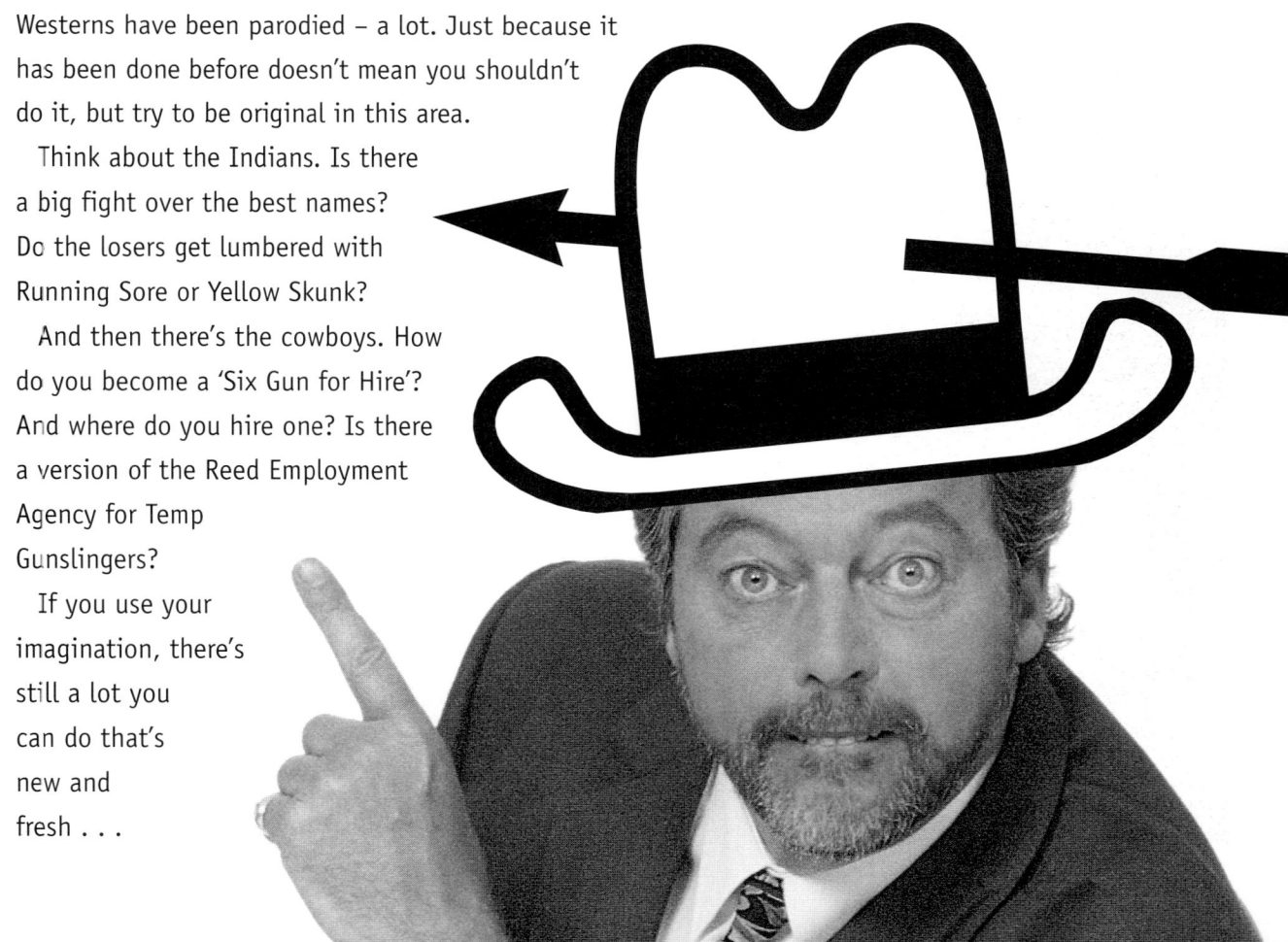

Sci-Fi

Science Fiction is a great area to parody – especially if you're a fan. There are just so many wonderful and bizarre concepts to turn into sketches – robots, time travel, grotesque alien races, interstellar empires, telepaths, spaceships, *Star Wars*, monsters. And outrageous TV shows . . .

Dr Who

It's a sitting duck. The BBC might not want to make *Dr Who* any more, but you probably do!

The joy is that, since the Doctor regenerates in a different body all the time, anyone can play him. Your lead actor is simply the next incarnation. He can wear pretty much anything, providing it's ridiculous enough. Don't forget to give him a companion, preferably a woman who likes screaming a lot and asks incredibly naïve questions, despite the fact that she's a top nuclear physicist. You won't find a police box to film by any more but, hey, maybe

the Doctor has moved with the times – or perhaps the 'Chameleon effect' is bust. Now it looks like a portaloo. Or a back garden shed. Or an Austin Metro. If the sound effect's right, people will accept it.

Make your own monsters – and think cheap. Stick paper clips to your face or put on one of those false nose and glasses sets and sellotape a small indoor TV aerial to your head. Go for the very worst effects you can. Pitch the Doctor against 'The Menace of the Cardboard Boxes' or 'Furniture of Doom'. Cheat: create 'The Terror of the Invisible Enemy'! Or 'My Scarf Possessed'! NB During your spoof, be sure to have your characters run up and down corridors a lot.

The Thing That Fell to Earth

It was lucky that David Bowie looked vaguely human in *The Man Who Fell to Earth*. Imagine if a *very* strange-looking alien ended up being marooned in Croydon with no hope of rescue. It would still have to eat, and meet humans. It might go shopping at Tesco and hang out in night clubs. You get the idea . . .

All you need is a creature mask. The very ordinariness of everything around the alien is actually a plus. You don't need sets or other special effects – just a very brave friend prepared to walk down Croydon High Street on a busy Saturday afternoon in a monster mask!

The Thing That Fell to Earth (and landed in the High Street)

Time travel

Modern attitudes meets costume drama. Once again, the fun is in putting ordinary people in extraordinary situations (and perhaps changing the course of future world events). This can involve 'ordinary' time travellers meeting great historical figures or weirdos from the future trying to blend in with our world.

Don't forget, you can go forward as well as back (and please, please, spare us that twist where you become your own grandfather!).

ALIEN INVASION

YOU MIGHT WANT TO PARODY THOSE FIFTIES 'B-MOVIES' WHERE THE YOUNG MILITARY MAN, THE SCIENTIST AND HIS BEAUTIFUL DAUGHTER SAVE THE PLANET FROM A BLOB/GIANT ANT/ARMY OF ALIENS/POD BEING/SPACE DINOSAUR/KILLER ROBOT/FORCE BEYOND IMAGINATION CREATED BY PUTTING A FUNNY LENS ON THE CAMERA. I REALLY DON'T NEED TO TELL YOU, DO I, THAT YOU CAN MAKE YOUR BLOCKBUSTER LOOK BLACK AND WHITE BY TURNING DOWN THE COLOUR ON YOUR TV SET? NO? GOOD.

Advertising Parodies

Most ads take themselves far too seriously. They promote their products like they were the most important thing in the world – and it's time to puncture their pomposity and take them down a peg or two. Advertising parodies are popular because everyone recognises them – and they're short and to the point.

Think of the ads which annoy you. Get your own back! Twist their message around. Inject the everyday into their glamorous world. Ask yourself what would really happen in some of those situations? These are some of the best (or worst, depending on your viewpoint): the Renault 'Nicole/Papa' series; the Nescafé Gold Blend saga; Hamlet cigars; Quality Street 'Magic Moments'; Ferrero Rocher; Cadbury's 'Flake'; 'Milk Tray' and 'Wash 'n' Go'.

GO'N'WASH

THE SHAMPOO FOR NEW AGE TRAVELLERS

OTHER TYPES OF COMMERCIALS RIPE FOR PARODY INCLUDE:
★ SOAP POWDERS AND THE DREADED DOORSTEP CHALLENGE
★ AFTER SHAVES AND COSMETICS
★ ALL THE BEERS CLAIMING TO BE IRISH
★ TWO WOMEN TALKING IN THE SUPERMARKET
★ MACHO SHAVING RAZORS

Sit-Coms

Parodying a sit-com is both simple and hard. The joy is that, most of the time, you can film it in your own house – no props or sets or locations needed. The hard part comes with the 'parody' bit. If you just do a sit-com about an everyday – or slightly kooky – family who live in a house, you're not parodying sit-com. You're just making another one. And if there's something the world doesn't need, it's yet another sit-com about a slightly kooky family living in a house.

To parody sit-com you've got to take the cliché and turn it at least sideways, if not on its head. Introduce elements that don't belong in the comfy world of suburbia:

Defrocked!

The Reverend Leslie Brown desperately wants a parish of his own, but all the new slots which become available are being given to new women priests in the interest of equal opportunities.

30

*So what do you think he does? Yes, he becomes Lesley Brown –
woman priest extraordinaire . . .*

My Cousin Saddam – or 'A Bit of a Coup'

*What happens on that fateful day when Saddam Hussein is finally
deposed and is forced into secretly fleeing Iraq? Well, fortunately for
him there is one place he can go – his distant cousin Malcolm's house
in leafy suburban England.*

*Once there, and without slaves, death squads and secret police,
Saddam finds English life exceptionally strange. He has enormous
problems even shopping in supermarkets, dealing with liberated
western women and working in his new job in the high street burger
bar (where he insists on wearing his full dress uniform) . . .*

Hang On In There

*Following the reintroduction of capital punishment in 1999 Britain
needs a new official hangman. Due to a bizarre administrative error,
the job goes to a TV game show host, Bruce Diamond, who stamps his
own unique identity on the post.*

Public executions have never been so much fun . . .

Documentaries

Spoof documentaries are fun – and they're relatively
simple for amateur film makers. They tend not to require
elaborate costumes, sets or props – and you can even get
away with some dodgy camerawork. Hand-held 'verité'
style filming – which we'll discuss later – suits this subject
perfectly. What's more, this is one time when your
characters can all hold a microphone in clear view, so
sound can be simplified as well.

What will you make your documentary about? Most
obviously, there's the Roger Cook style of dramatic
investigative telly journalism. You can pretty much
'expose' anything – stupid crime syndicates;
scandalous products being foisted on an unsuspecting

POLICE +
CAMERA +
CHASE +
CRASH =
Boosted TV ratings
New for the BBC
starts Tuesday

Around the World of Leather in 80 Days

With Michael 'Just Looking' Palin

public; pets which unaccountably explode for no reason.

Don't forget, however, that there's more to documentaries than the 'exposé'. Why not make a David Attenborough-style wildlife documentary about your pets or your Uncle Fred, who's a bit odd and smelly and unkempt . . .

Travel shows can be documentaries too. Imagine making your own version of *Michael Palin's Full Circle* – but on a considerably smaller budget. What sort of travelogue could you produce with a one-day bus pass and a packed lunch?

Soap Operas

Soap operas are a particularly good area for Blockbuster makers because they feature ordinary people in ordinary surroundings. No need for costumes, elaborate props, locations or special effects. No need for good acting either.

Anyone can do an Australian accent and anyone can parody an Australian soap opera. So what if you haven't got a surfboard – you've got an ironing board haven't you? Throw some tinnies on the barbie (on second thoughts – don't do that!) and come up with the most outrageous plot you can think of.

Who knows? You may even want to make several 'episodes' of your own soap opera, with events getting ever more stupid and unbelievable.

You don't have to do Australian soaps of course. You could create your own version of *EastEnders* or *Coronation Street* or *Brookside* too, either with your impersonations of Deirdre and Bianca or with totally new characters. Or you could create your own soap from scratch based in Romford or Chester or wherever you live. The rules are the same in every case. Be outrageous and unbelievable!

Horror Movies

Carry On Screaming, the *Rocky Horror Picture Show* and *Young Frankenstein*, *The Addams Family* and *The Munsters*; *Abbot and Costello Meet The Wolfman* and *Love At First Bite*: horror parodies have been done to death – and beyond. But that won't stop you because making a horror Blockbuster is so much fun. You get to put on great make-up. You get to do crazy special effects. You get to sink your teeth into the necks of beautiful women (and they don't press charges).

Other Areas We Haven't Touched On

They're out of vogue at the moment, but war movies provide a great source of parody. Think of the Smith and Jones sketch where they featured all the different cliché German officers, or the Monty Python sketch in which Battle of Britain Spitfire pilots couldn't understand each other's slang. There was even a very short-lived sit-com called *Heil Honey, I'm Home* which featured Adolf Hitler and his girlfriend Eva Braun in the style of *I Love Lucy*!

The Vampire Cricket XI in BAT OUT OF HELL

We haven't really looked at musicals either, because of the obvious production difficulties. Can you write music and lyrics? Can your troupe of Thespians sing or play musical instruments? If not, it's probably better to settle for a mimed performance of 'You're The One That I Want' or 'Bless Your Beautiful Hide'. Come on, Uncle Derek sort of looks like Howard Keel, if you keep the lights off him and stand him on a box and have something done about all those warts . . .

If you and your mates are a multi-talented lot and you can create your own musical, try to make it about an unusual subject that no one's ever written about before. Is the world really ready for 'Gandhi – the Musical', or the world's first comic opera about the Black Death? Probably not – but don't let that stop you!

Being naughty . . . Hidden Camera Capers

Of course, you'd expect me to recommend these! The first rule of playing a practical joke on someone is that they've got to be able to take it. Don't pick on the vulnerable or elderly – or someone with a hair-trigger temper and a collection of antique shotguns. Secondly, don't break the law or damage anything in your zeal to pull the perfect practical joke. That means no breaking into people's houses to plant cameras, or driving their prized Ford Puma into a swimming pool just to capture their reaction.

REMOTE CONTROL

OBVIOUSLY, YOU CAN'T START ON YOUR PRACTICAL JOKE AND THEN BREAK AWAY SAYING, 'JUST LET ME TURN THE HIDDEN CAMERA ON!' IF YOU'VE GOT A REMOTE CONTROL FACILITY ON YOUR CAMCORDER, NOW'S THE TIME TO USE IT. DON'T WORRY IF YOU HAVEN'T. YOU CAN ALWAYS TURN THE CAMERA ON AND THEN LEAD YOUR 'VICTIM' INTO THE ROOM. FOR SOME PRANKS YOU CAN ACTUALLY HAVE SOMEONE OPERATING THE CAMCORDER FOR YOU.

Locations

The easiest place to pull a stunt is in your own home, because you've got control of everything and you can set things up in advance. Other than that, you might like to consider the garden or in a 'neutral' area. It can be very difficult to set up a hidden camera stunt in someone else's house without their knowledge – and they might feel more upset about it than if you caught them out at their own place.

What prank?

At first, keep your pranks very simple. You can progress to more outrageous ones as your skill and confidence improves.

You know what your friends are likely to fall for and what they won't. Build on that. Build on their interests, their desires and their ambitions.

Your hidden camera prank can be anything from the always dependable jumping out of a cupboard and yelling 'boo!' to more sophisticated stunts. 'Wind up' conversations work very well, because they tend to keep your target static in front of the camcorder. Ask them to invest £10,000 in your new connoisseur cheese pyramid-selling scheme – or confess you were once a woman. Ask for a loan to cover a sex change operation, tell them about your alien abduction experiences or get them to audition for the new singing act you're planning. Be careful though. It's no fun to suggest an outrageous partner-swapping night with your best mate as a joke – only to find he eagerly agrees with you!

Setting Up Your Hidden Camera

You can position the camcorder on almost any flat, secure surface, preferably at head height. It might be hidden amongst books or videos, ornaments or crockery etc. The only parts that need to be unobscured are the lens and the microphone (unless you're using an external mic).

Think about where your 'victim' is going to be standing and position the camcorder to capture them perfectly. The easiest way to anticipate this is if you are planning a 'face to face' chat with them. The camcorder shoots over your shoulder and captures all their expressions.

You can film out of a car but beware of autofocus and reflection problems if the window is closed. You'll also need a radio microphone if you want to catch what's being said.

You can hide a camcorder inside a handbag or shoulder bag – but you'll need to cut a hole for the lens to see through. It's very hard to control what kind of shots you'll get, especially without considerable

Beadle Tips

★ IF YOU CAN, TEST EVERYTHING IN ADVANCE. SET UP THE CAMERA, USE A 'STAND IN' FOR YOUR 'VICTIM' AND RECORD THE SCENE. MAKE SURE THAT YOUR VICTIM IS FACING THE CAMCORDER AT ALL TIMES AND THAT THE SOUND IS CLEAR.

★ REMEMBER THAT THE FLASHING RED LIGHT ON A CAMCORDER CAN BE A DEAD GIVEAWAY. STICK INSULATING TAPE OVER IT SO IT CAN'T BE SEEN.

practice, but it will enable you to play jokes in places where you can't otherwise plant a hidden camera, like shops for example.

My Favourite Hidden Camera Prank

Just before you host a party, take your camcorder and a stepladder into your toilet. Get the camcorder up high near the ceiling, as if it were a security camera and film the empty toilet for about five minutes.

Now, during the party, your intended victim leaves to go to the toilet. When they come back, the TV is on and you're playing the video you shot earlier – of the empty toilet. Of course, they panic and assume you've been secretly taping them 'live' in there! Your guests, who are in on the joke, start to wind up the victim, getting them madder and madder: 'Shall we wind it back and watch it again? What on earth were you doing? Would you like a copy?'

The real joke is, of course, that you're now filming their explosive reactions 'live' on a camcorder hidden in the room!

The Man in the Street

At your own peril, you might like to pretend to be a real documentary team and stop strangers in the street to ask them questions, just like a real life investigative journalist. You can then cut these into a broader documentary spoof you're making – or make an entire sketch of it! The secret is to keep a straight face – and not to ask a six foot four navvy when he's going to drop the act and come out of the closet . . .

Wind people up by telling them outrageous porkies about the EU. Tell them that Brussels is planning legislation to make all bath plugs square – or letter boxes the same Euro size. Ask them to sign a petition against the EU's plan to replace our National Anthem with a Euro Anthem sung by puppet mouse Topo Gigio. People believe anything about the EU and – as the old saying goes – 'Bull Baffles Brains'. If you can keep a straight face, and you start from a plausible premise like a European directive, you can get sillier and sillier and you'll still get away with it!

PRACTICAL JOKES

VIDEOING PEOPLE'S REACTIONS TO SIMPLE PRANKS IS EASY AND PARTICULARLY FUNNY IF YOU EDIT A WHOLE SEQUENCE OF THEM TOGETHER: THINGS LIKE STICKING A POUND COIN TO THE PAVEMENT WITH SUPERGLUE; GOING UP TO SOMEONE AND TELLING THEM THEIR FLIES ARE UNDONE – AND CAPTURING THEIR REACTION; LOOKING UP AND POINTING AT THE SKY, SEEING HOW MANY OTHER PEOPLE JOIN YOU – EVEN GOING UP TO SOMEONE IN THE STREET SMILING WITH YOUR ARMS OUTSTRETCHED – AND THEN WALKING PAST THEM TO GREET A FRIEND (SOMEONE YOU KNOW) WHO'S WALKING RIGHT BEHIND THEM.

YOU COULD EVEN PUT THESE TO A SOUND TRACK. HOW ABOUT THE WHO'S 'WON'T GET FOOLED AGAIN' OR CHRIS REA'S 'FOOL IF YOU THINK IT'S OVER'?

Still Stuck for Ideas?

D on't worry! Not everyone is born to be a TV comedy writer. That's why those who write TV comedy professionally are paid such huge sums of money. (That's a joke by the way.) If you're really stuck for ideas, try one of the following methods.

★ Start cutting cartoons out of newspapers and magazines. After a while, you'll see that you may have several on a particular theme. Perhaps it's fishing, or traffic wardens or car mechanics or shopping or life in the office. Lay them out and – hey presto – you've got a storyboard of sorts. Put the best gag at the end, the second best gag at the beginning and you're on the way to building up your own sketch. You take the jokes, convert them into a script and you're ready to go!

★ Collect old greetings cards. Most of them have the set-up to a joke on the cover – and a ready-made punchline inside.

★ Perform your own version of someone else's sketch. Admit it, you'd pay good money to see Uncle Albert and Cousin Frank re-creating 'The Ministry of Silly Walks' or performing 'The Parrot Sketch'. Look in the humour section of your local bookshop or library for collections of well-known TV sketches, or buy a video and then write out the sketch yourself. Is it legal? Hmmm. Probably not. After all, that's someone else's hard

Beadle's 'Did You Know?'

THIS IS HOW BENNY HILL CREATED MANY OF HIS SKETCHES. IF IT WAS GOOD ENOUGH FOR HIM, IT'S GOOD ENOUGH FOR YOU!

work you're using. But if you're only making it for your own amusement and not intending to charge people to see it or claim that you wrote it, it's hard to imagine you'll have much grief. If you're genuinely stuck for ideas and finding it hard to get going, this method can teach you a lot. You'll see how the sketch has been constructed and – if you've got it on tape – how the director chose to film it. You can follow his shots or change them. It's up to you. After you've remade a few classic sketches, you'll know a lot more about writing and filming your own. Then you can get original!

★ Get someone else to create your Blockbuster for you. It's no shame. Alfred Hitchcock was a great director – but he never claimed to be a writer. His job was to turn someone else's idea into a finished film. Ask your friends and family to come up with ideas and – when you hear one you like – take it up as your project (remembering to give them a full credit!).

★ Turn a joke into a sketch. Come on, you know plenty of jokes, so in theory you have plenty of sketch ideas already in your head. Obviously, some jokes won't convert to a sketch as well as others – and some are probably too blue to be filmed legally – but in many jokes you have a ready made sketch. Best of all, jokes have a punchline. There it is – your sketch – already written for you. All you have to do is figure out how to film it.

Here's a joke:

A lawyer arrives at the Pearly Gates and is given a very warm welcome by St Peter. This surprises the lawyer, who didn't expect such a reception because of his profession. He asks St Peter why he's being so nice. St Peter tells him that it's not often they get someone of his very advanced years. The lawyer is confused. 'But I'm only 48!' he says. St Peter consults a thick wad of papers and says, 'That's odd. From all those hours you've billed we thought you must be 140!'

Now, here's how that joke might be turned into a shooting script, using some local cemetery gates to stand in for the Pearly Gates...

'THE ONLY GOOD LAWYER…'

<u>EXT</u>   PEARLY GATES

ST PETER IS STANDING IN FRONT OF THE PEARLY GATES HOLDING
A THICK SHEAF OF PAPER AND WEARING A WHITE GOWN

<u>SOUND:</u>   <u>HEAVENLY MUSIC</u>

THE LAWYER WALKS INTO SHOT IN HIS PYJAMAS, LOOKING DAZED
AND CONFUSED

ST PETER
Welcome to heaven, my son.

LAWYER
I 'm dead? I'm in heaven?

ST PETER
(Matter of factly) Yes… I just need to check a few facts.

ST PETER CONSULTS HIS PAPERS

ST PETER
(Pleasantly surprised) Oh Mr Jarvis! Hello! Welcome.
We're really thrilled to have you here!

LAWYER
(Equally surprised) You are?

ST PETER
Most definitely. This is a real honour for us.

LAWYER
But I'm a lawyer! I never expected to end up here
(GESTURES AROUND) let alone get this sort of welcome…

ST PETER
All of Heaven is celebrating. It's not every day
that we receive someone of your advanced years.

LAWYER
(Confused) But I'm only 48!

ST PETER FROWNS AND HURRIED CONSULTS HIS WAD OF PAPERS

ST PETER
Oh… From all these hours you've billed we thought
you were 140.

Get the idea?

Writing a Comedy Script

After the initial idea, the most important part of your comedy video is your script.

Your audience will forgive bad sets (especially if they were fans of *Crossroads* or *Neighbours*) and bad acting (ditto). These might even add to the charm and fun of your video. However, the same people will be your fiercest critics if the script is bad.

Give me a good script and I'll be a hundred times better as a director

George Cukor, director of *The Philadelphia Story, A Star Is Born* **and** *My Fair Lady*

I couldn't agree more

Jeremy Beadle

You'd be surprised at the number of people I meet making comedy videos who get bogged down in technique and technicalities. They put all their time and effort into making sure their video looks and sounds good – but forget that the fundamental objective of a comedy video is to make people laugh, not get them to appreciate balanced lighting or a well-composed long shot.

So, how do you write a good comedy script? Well the good news is that you don't have to be born with the Funny Gene, nor do you have to trek to a remote Himalayan peak to gain an insight and knowledge of 'how to be funny' from some Tibetan Holy Man.

No. Writing comedy scripts is a craft rather than an art, based on learning from techniques that are tried and tested. (Of course, it helps if you've got a pretty good idea of what's funny and what isn't, a good imagination and a basic ability to put your thoughts and ideas down in writing.)

Beadle's 10 Golden Rules for Writing a Comedy Script (Apart from 'Make it Funny')

Rule 1: Know your audience

If you're making a video just for your own and your friends' enjoyment then you'll probably choose a subject you can all relate to, no matter how specialised (i.e. 'obscure') it might be – for example, a hilarious look at your Morris Minor's chassis or a video about the odd teachers you had at school. However, if you want to present your video to a wider audience then you need to have a script with a much broader appeal.

In addition, be wary of using bad language (not everyone is as broadminded as you) and attempting to make a black comedy (your audience might not have a high appreciation of irony). You might have every good intention of using humour to make a necessary social comment about racism, disability, chronic illness or religion but, unless you have a sympathetic understanding of the subject and good script writing skills, you run the risk of appearing racist, sexist, bigoted, sick, perverted – or all of them simultaneously.

At the end of the day, although your audience probably hasn't paid to see your video, they're still expecting something funny. Your task is to make sure they're not disappointed.

Rule 2: Familiarity is funny

People like strong, well-fleshed characters they can instantly recognise (and sometimes identify with). Look at some of the best sit-coms. They're the ones with the strongest characterisations – *Men Behaving Badly*, *Absolutely Fabulous*, *Dad's Army*, *Fawlty Towers*, *Only Fools and Horses*, *Steptoe & Son*, *The Good Life*, *Frasier*, *Hancock*, *Bilko*, *Friends*, *Cheers*, *Are You Being Served?* etc.

Now a lot of these characters are what I call 'Cliché+'. By this I mean that the writers have accentuated their traits to a degree that takes the characters from just being amusing or endearing to being truly funny.

Take the middle-class, middle-aged bank manager with a misplaced snobbery (Captain Mainwaring) or the camp, provocative, teasing men's-wear assistant (Mr Humphries).

No one is that extreme in real life (apart from people

working in television, but that's another story) and it's this exaggeration that makes them work so well. (In any case, the chances are that your cast won't be able to play their roles too subtly – this doesn't matter because you can get laughs from over-acting!)

Rule 3: Establish the characters as soon as possible

It's important that your audience understands who your characters are as early as possible. For example, if a scientist is mad, don't present him as a logical, rational professional and then suddenly reveal that he's one test tube short of a chemistry set. For maximum effect, you should make it clear what he's all about on his first appearance. He should look and act like a cross between Einstein, Dr Magnus Pike and Christopher Lloyd from *Back to the Future*.

Rule 4: Get your laughs from both the situations and the characters

A man who's got the shakes is funny, but put him in the situation where he's trying to defuse an unexploded bomb and he's funnier. Equally, a blue comedian is also a funny character but can be even funnier when he finds himself at a formal banquet or a children's party, desperately trying to clean up his act (and failing).

I said before that your characters can be larger than life. That's fine – just make sure that the characters themselves don't realise they behave in an extreme way. For all intents and purposes they should think they're normal. Mel Brooks once said that: 'Comedy is serious – deadly serious. Never, never try to be funny! The actors must be serious. Only the situation must be absurd.' And who am I, a humble top international television presenter, to argue with him?

Rule 5: Keep it moving

Comedy, like your creative juices, should flow. If you're struggling to get a laugh from a situation and there's a long set-up to get there, leave it out. If you take too long setting up a joke the audience will get bored or, worse still, predict the outcome, and the gag will suffer.

SCRIPT LAYOUT

THERE ARE INDUSTRY-ACCEPTED SCRIPT LAYOUTS FOR TV SHOWS, COMMERCIALS AND MOVIES, WITH STANDARDS FOR SPACING, USE OF CAPITAL LETTERS AND UNDERLINING, POSITION OF TEXT ON THE PAGE ETC. HOWEVER THIS SORT OF DETAIL ISN'T IMPORTANT. WHAT IS IMPORTANT IS THAT YOUR SCRIPT CLEARLY SEPARATES YOUR PERFORMERS' DIALOGUE AND ACTIONS FROM THE TYPE OF SHOTS REQUIRED (WHICH IS MAINLY OF USE JUST TO THE DIRECTOR AND/OR PERSON FILMING). COPY THE LAYOUT ON P.39 IF IT SUITS YOU.

THE SCREENWRITER'S STORE IN LONDON SELLS VARIOUS SCRIPTWRITING SOFTWARE THAT DOES ALL THE FORMATTING FOR YOU. CHECK OUT THEIR WEBSITE: http://www.screenwriterstore.co.uk/

Rule 6: Make sure every effect has a cause

It might sound obvious but apart from any influence from the supernatural, nothing happens without a reason. Even in comedy Blockbusters.

Water bursts out of a pipe because someone's hammered a nail in it; people trip up because something's in the way. Cars roll down hills because the hand-brake has been knocked off.

These things don't happen by themselves so, when you're writing your script, you'll need to hint earlier on at the reason for some later event taking place – someone's clumsy, someone has a messy house (just don't make it too contrived).

Rule 7: Keep it short and sweet

How long is a good comedy video? Long enough to tell the story that leads to a satisfying conclusion but short enough to have pace and remain funny. It goes without saying that if a sequence or a scene isn't that funny, take it out.

You won't get any acclaim for making a comedy epic that's long in length but short on laughs.

Rule 8: Try to obey the 'rule of three'

Ideally, each line of comic dialogue should contain a joke or set up a joke – but that's pushing it. Sit-com writers try and adhere to 'The Rule Of Three' – that is, that every third line should contain a joke. This is very hard to attain (most sit-com writers don't even manage 'The Rule of Eight') but it's a worthy goal to strive for!

Rule 9: Have a punchline!

Also called a 'tag', this is the natural climax to a joke and might be delivered verbally or visually. To be effective, a punchline should be unexpected but not necessarily surreal. Monty Python got away with that because their audience came to accept (and expect) this. Saying 'This sketch is getting silly' and leaving it, or 'Now for something completely different' became a handy get-out to any sketch that couldn't be resolved.

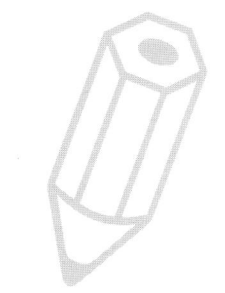

SCRIPT TERMS AND ABBREVIATIONS
THESE ARE THE MOST COMMON DESCRIPTIONS AND ABBREVIATIONS YOU'LL NEED FOR A SCRIPT (DON'T WORRY ABOUT THE DIFFERENT TYPES OF SHOTS – YOU'LL FIND THEM EXPLAINED ON P.46):

CU	CLOSE-UP
ECU	EXTREME CLOSE-UP
EXT	EXTERIOR LOCATION
INT	INTERIOR LOCATION
LS	LONG SHOT
MS	MEDIUM SHOT
N/S	NO SOUND
O/C	OFF CAMERA (ANY ACTION OR SOUND THAT TAKES PLACE OFF SCREEN)
POV	POINT OF VIEW
SUPER	A SUPERIMPOSED CAPTION OR IMAGE (USUALLY A STILL)
VO	VOICE OVER (A NARRATOR SPEAKING OVER THE FILMED ACTION)

Coming up with the punchline is the hardest part. Sometimes you've got a great idea for a comedy set piece. It builds up with some really good lines and exchanges but then what you thought was the road to a triumphant finish looks destined for a Comedy Cul-de-Sac. (In this case, there's no substitute for working at it. If it's any consolation, it sometimes takes professional comedy writers as long to come up with the punchline as it does to write the rest of the script.)

If you're lucky, you might already have an idea of what the punchline will be before you start writing. Then it's a question of working backwards from there.

Rule 10: Don't telegraph a punchline

Punchlines to jokes and set-ups shouldn't be so obvious that when they do eventually happen, the audience has already anticipated them. For example, one set-up might be a thief dressed as a clown breaking into a museum to steal a precious vase (the reason he's dressed as a clown was explained in an earlier scene. Honest). The gag here is that to steal the vase, the clown must lie on his back and shimmy along the floor, under a light beam that's connected to the alarm. He's tense, sweating profusely. He breathes in to make his fat clown stomach as flat as possible, missing the beam by a hair's breadth. All goes well except he forgets he's wearing clown shoes – about two feet long – and they break the beam.

The way to film this would be shots of him edging along, inter-cut with close-ups of the light beam and the sweat on his brow. We'd see him sucking in to reduce his stomach until he literally can't breathe any more, but you wouldn't reveal the big clown boots until the alarm sounds.

The *wrong* way would be to emphasise his long shoes, that is, you show them approaching the beam, getting nearer and nearer until the alarm goes off. There is still a joke here (why didn't the thief take off his ridiculous shoes in the first place?) but the audience knows what will happen well in advance.

This is called 'telegraphing' a punchline (that is, you tell everyone about it long before it arrives).

You and Your Camcorder

Never be afraid to experiment with your camcorder. Try out lots of different things. Try all the buttons. Play with your camcorder. Shoot anything and everything – people, places, objects, action, the sky. Anything, just to get a feel for how they look. Try out the zoom at different speeds too (see pp.53-54).

The more you use your camcorder, the more mistakes you make, and the quicker you learn.

Get to Know Your Camcorder Better

The better you know your camcorder, the more you'll be able to do with it and the better the results you'll get. There are two ways of getting to know your camcorder. You can take it to the movies or to expensive restaurants and then spend time alone together in front of a roaring open fire, exploring each other's hopes and dreams – or you can read the instruction manual.

The wrong way to get to know your camcorder better...

Guess which method works.

Go on – find it. You know you saw it somewhere. Was it down the back of the refrigerator, covered in jam stains, or in the shed behind the motor mower, sopping up the sump oil? You didn't really read it when you had it, did you? You don't know what all those fussy little buttons do, do you? You learned just enough to make the camera work and then you wanted to go and play with your new toy so you flung that manual aside and forgot all about it.

Take the time to read it. You'll probably find your camcorder is capable of far more than you think. That means shooting and editing your Blockbuster may be easier – and you'll be able to achieve effects you never dreamed of!

A Close-Up Look at Types of Shots

Beadle Tips

★ DON'T USE TOO MANY CLOSE-UPS OR YOUR AUDIENCE WILL FORGET WHAT'S GOING ON AROUND THE PERFORMER. YOU'LL NEED TO SWITCH BACK TO WIDER SHOTS WHEN SOMETHING NEW HAPPENS, FOR EXAMPLE WHEN SOMEONE COMES INTO THE ROOM, OR PRODUCES AN AARDVARK FROM THEIR TROUSERS – OR WHATEVER.

★ GIVE ALL THE ACTORS IN YOUR PRODUCTION THEIR OWN CLOSE-UP, NO MATTER HOW SMALL THEIR PART IS. THEY ALL DESERVE IT!

OK. So you've had your big idea and you've written your script. Now it's time to replace your scriptwriter's hat with your director's hat. I mean this metaphorically of course. Although there's nothing to stop you wearing a big hat with the word 'Director' written on it, if you so wish (just make sure it's your colour and it's not too tight).

Choosing the right types of shots will bring your script to life. They will enhance your production and make a good video a great one. You could have a really funny script but the wrong type of shot can, at best, lessen the impact of a particular gag or, at worst, ruin it completely.

These are the main types of shots film directors use. (Yes, I know there are others but I'm trying to keep it simple. Remember, this isn't a book for anoraks, OK?)

Point-of-View Shot (POV)

This isn't a specific type of shot, but rather a technique, used so that the viewer can identify with a particular character – and literally see through his or her eyes. Suppose your beautiful heroine is being chased through some woods by a ghastly, horrible monster. For this you would take her position and hand-hold your camcorder as you walk/run/stumble through the trees. To show her stopping and looking round – you do the same. If she looks to her right, your camcorder moves to the right and so on. With a POV shot it's acceptable to have some degree of jerkiness – it makes the shot more realistic. Equally, if she falls over – you do the same (trying not to damage your camcorder in the process).

Remember that animals and children have different points-of-view and shooting from their viewpoint should be considered. How about something like 'A Day In The Life Of My Cocker Spaniel' – with the story told (and filmed) from the dog's perspective?

The 'Cut-Away'

Cut-aways are brief shots that take you temporarily away from the main action. They can be used to break up shots that are either too long or too similar to each other. They can help you to draw the audience's attention to important little details, like that time bomb ticking away in the cupboard, or the tin tack on the chair, just waiting to be sat on.

Cut-aways can also be used to good comedy effect – to show what's known as 'parallel action' – action that's going on simultaneously with the scene you're watching. This lets your audience enjoy seeing something and knowing something that the main characters don't. The audience loves to anticipate what's going to happen and you can use this to build to a great comic climax.

Long Shot (LS)
Used as an establishing shot, to set the scene. The shot could be of a person, a road, a house, a landscape – anything really (even a couch in a living room)

Medium Shot or Mid-Shot (MS)
This shot focuses your attention on something in particular (in this case, a group of cuddly soft toys)

Close-Up (CU)
Used to make your audience concentrate on a specific part of the scene or one person (or in this case, Big Ted)

Extreme Close-Up (ECU)
Used to draw attention to something like an expression, an object or a distinguishing feature, like a threadbare nose

Common Problems When Directing

The jump cut

You're looking at two characters in the distance walking towards you. Then, in the very next shot, they're suddenly two feet away from you. How did they do this? Did they suddenly teleport the missing distance? Possibly, but it's much more likely that the director has committed a cardinal sin called a jump cut.

He's left out a piece of continuous action and the audience can't understand where it's gone. In their eyes, the characters have 'jumped'. Even the smallest jump cut still jars.

One way to avoid a jump cut is to shoot the action continuously. If this is just too long and boring, there are ways to speed up the passing of time:

★Use a mix or a fade in and out to suggest time passing between the shots – see p.49.

★Use cut-aways, as above.

★Use radically different shots: break up long shots with close-ups to disguise the passing of time.

Audiences are so used to seeing these 'cheats' that they accept them without question.

If you film anywhere within this 180° arc, your subject will always appear to be travelling in the same direction

The 180° rule

Don't go near the water. Don't rock on those chairs. Don't pick your nose. All good, sound pieces of advice and to those sage words I'd add the following pearl of wisdom for video makers: Don't Cross The Line!

What does it mean? Well, suppose you're filming someone walking from left to right using a number of different shots. If you imagine they're walking along an invisible line, then you can film from anywhere within a 180° arc forward of this line, *as long as you do not **cross** the line.*

What happens if you cross the line? Well you won't disappear into another dimension, or anything like that, but when you come to edit your video you'll discover that sometimes your subject is walking left to right and sometimes right to left. Cut these together and your audience won't know if the subject is coming or going.

Maintaining eye-lines

Two people looking at each other must maintain the same position of their heads – and, therefore, their eyes. Imagine you're filming 'Confessions of a Roof Tiler'. In your establishing shot you might see someone up a ladder talking to his mate on the ground. One of them would naturally be looking down – and the other would be looking up. If you use close-up shots of both men in conversation then make sure you keep their eye-line – i.e. the man up the ladder should always look down. If he looks straight ahead or upwards, the audience will be confused (and rightly so).

Other things you ought to know about:

Fade: This is where a shot darkens gradually until it's completely black – to indicate the end of a scene (or the whole video). Sometimes you'll see one shot fade down and a different shot fade up from darkness. This is used to indicate time passing.

Wipe: A rather drastic way of changing scene where a new scene literally pushes the old one off the screen. It can do this horizontally, vertically or in any one of a number of ways.

Mix/Dissolve: The effect where a new shot suddenly starts to emerge while the old shot is still on the screen. The old shot slowly fades out and is replaced completely by the new one. Fast mixes make for an elegant transition between shots. Slower ones suggest time is passing between the two events.

Verité: Filming with no tripod and no real consideration for preventing camera shake. This is the style you want to use if you're pastiching a TV news team in the thick of things, desperately trying to tape what's going on around them with no pre-planning beforehand. Think of Roger Cook.

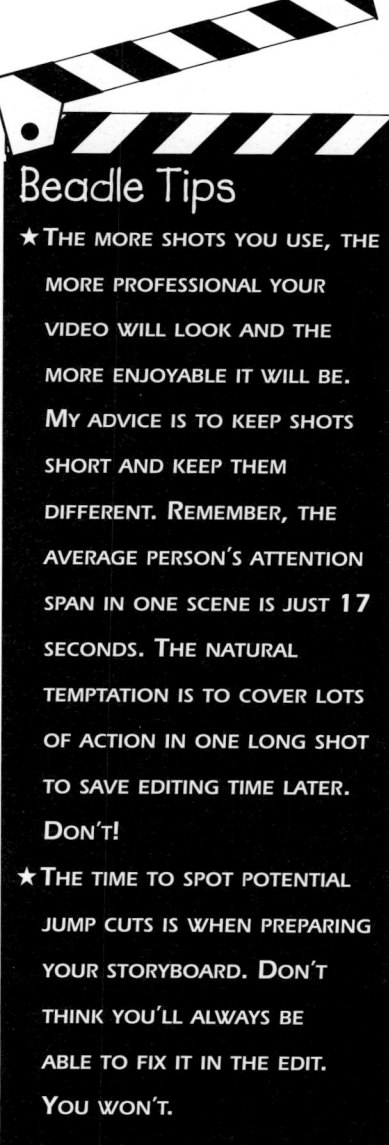

Beadle Tips

★ THE MORE SHOTS YOU USE, THE MORE PROFESSIONAL YOUR VIDEO WILL LOOK AND THE MORE ENJOYABLE IT WILL BE. MY ADVICE IS TO KEEP SHOTS SHORT AND KEEP THEM DIFFERENT. REMEMBER, THE AVERAGE PERSON'S ATTENTION SPAN IN ONE SCENE IS JUST 17 SECONDS. THE NATURAL TEMPTATION IS TO COVER LOTS OF ACTION IN ONE LONG SHOT TO SAVE EDITING TIME LATER. DON'T!

★ THE TIME TO SPOT POTENTIAL JUMP CUTS IS WHEN PREPARING YOUR STORYBOARD. DON'T THINK YOU'LL ALWAYS BE ABLE TO FIX IT IN THE EDIT. YOU WON'T.

Panning, Tilting, Tracking, Zooming etc.

I t can be very confusing – we've all heard these terms, and we'd all probably recognise the effects, but it's easy to get mixed up between them. Let's look at what they're used for and how you can do them.

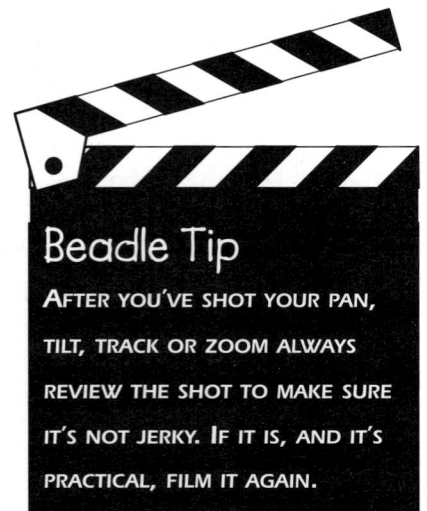

Beadle Tip

AFTER YOU'VE SHOT YOUR PAN, TILT, TRACK OR ZOOM ALWAYS REVIEW THE SHOT TO MAKE SURE IT'S NOT JERKY. IF IT IS, AND IT'S PRACTICAL, FILM IT AGAIN.

Panning

Keep still and swivel the camcorder horizontally in a wide arc. Pans are used to establish a location, to follow action or reveal new information in a scene.

★Wherever possible, pan with a tripod.

★Swivel smoothly without hesitating – changing your speed will just make the picture jerky.

★Hold your shot for a few seconds before and after your pan. This will ensure you have enough flexibility when editing.

★Keep your horizon level.

★Don't pan too fast. You might feel your pan is taking ages and ages but don't be tempted to speed it up. You'll be surprised at how fast the action moves when you view the finished shot.

★When following moving action, leave space in the frame in front of the object.

★Make sure your pan ends on something interesting – if possible, something that leads into the next shot – otherwise your audience will feel cheated.

★Don't overuse the move by constantly panning over a scene from left to right – then back again. This is known as 'hosepiping' since it's the same move you use to water a garden. Before you start videoing, impose your own hosepipe ban!

★A pan over a landscape where nothing's happening is called a 'static pan'. These make for seriously dull shots so the shorter, the better (better still, don't use them!).

Tilting

Think of this as a vertical pan; you stand still but tilt your camcorder up or down. Tilts can be used to stress the height of an object, to heighten suspense or just to reveal part of a scene.

★Wherever possible, tilt with a tripod.

★A comic effect is to start on a shot of someone's feet and then tilt upwards until you reach their head. This will make them look very tall or very menacing.

★Practise your tilt before you actually film – otherwise you might find yourself misjudging the height of a building and ending up toppling backwards, trying to fit the top storey in.

★As with panning, always hold your camcorder stationary for about three seconds before and after your tilt.

★Most tilts, because of their subjects, will include shots of the sky. If this is the case, keep an eye on the exposure.

Beadle Tip

WHIP PANS OR ZIP PANS. MUCH BELOVED OF BATMAN OR THE MAN FROM UNCLE, THESE ARE HIGH-SPEED PANS USED TO LINK TWO SCENES – USUALLY TO THE ACCOMPANIMENT OF DRAMATIC MUSIC. THEY'RE ACHIEVED BY WHIPPING THE CAMERA ROUND VERY, VERY FAST AT THE END OF ONE SCENE – THEN DOING THE SAME TO ENTER THE NEXT SCENE.

Tracking

Tracking can be two motions – moving your camcorder parallel to the action (also called 'crabbing') or moving it towards or away from the action (also known as 'dollying'). Tracking shots are mainly used to follow action, but unlike panning both you and your camcorder physically move. This gives the impression that the viewer is right there alongside the action.

Above: Tracking – parallel to subject

Professionals have it easy. Miniature 'railway' tracks are laid along a pre-determined route in advance. The camera and operator are situated on a platform that glides smoothly along the tracks, pulled/pushed by someone else. Amateurs don't have this luxury. Not only don't they have miniature railway tracks at their disposal, they may not even have 'someone else'. That means they must improvise – but can still achieve an effective shot.

Below: Tracking – to and from subject

★Some tripods come with optional wheels to allow you to do your own tracking shots. If you don't have this luxury, you can always clamp the tripod legs to a piece of board to which you've attached pram wheels.

★Other ways to track a shot are by filming from an armchair or office chair on castors, a wheelchair, a wheelbarrow or even a supermarket trolley. You sit comfortably (or as comfortably as you can in a supermarket trolley) while a helper pushes or pulls you to or from the action.

★If you're tracking back, make sure you know what's behind you – an ornamental pond, a busy road, a reversing dustcart etc.

Improvise! An office chair on castors can be used for an effective tracking shot

★Use the widest angle on your lens that you can; this will help minimise the effect of camera shake.

★You can also improvise a tracking shot by filming from a very slow-moving car – either with your head stuck out of the side window, the sunroof, or by sitting in the luggage compartment of a hatchback. Whatever method you use, make sure you use a quiet side street. Also, be wary of engine noise. If the car is small enough your 'crew' can push it while someone else steers.

Zooming

Zooming is filming while pressing the zoom lens rocker button, changing from wide angle to telephoto (or reverse). This has the effect of making your subject larger or smaller in the frame.

53

Zooming tips

★Remember that nothing on our planet changes its vision the way a zoom lens works and that alone is reason enough to use the effect as little as possible – if at all.

★As a guide, work out how many zoom shots you intend using in your video and halve them, then take away two. Too many zooms distract the viewer from what's going on.

★Shots that rapidly zoom in and out are pretty pointless and can make viewers feel ill (for obvious reasons, this nausea-inducing effect is known as 'tromboning'. If you use this technique you should join an orchestra, rather than make videos).

★The exception to rapid zooming in and out would be if you were making a parody of a British 1960s film, the type that involved a photographer, loads of girls in knee-length white leather boots and dresses with big circles on them, an E-type Jag, bad dialogue, David Hemmings and a sound track by the Tremeloes. Here you can zoom in and out to your heart's content, secure in the knowledge that an appreciative audience will recognise your parody – although the less aware will just think you've gone off your rocker (switch).

★Wherever possible, combine your zoom with another camera move – for instance, pan and zoom at the same time, or tilt and zoom. This will make your shot more interesting and will help to disguise the zoom.

★Always try and zoom using a tripod. With your zoom lens in its most extreme telephoto setting it's very unlikely you can hold the camcorder still enough to avoid camera shake.

Why zoom?

Good question. To be honest there aren't that many times when you need to zoom in to a subject. It's best limited to beginning your video; perhaps open on a group of people or buildings and zoom towards your subject to establish them. In comedy, you might want a very fast zoom in or out to reveal the punchline to a joke.

Beadle Tip

WHETHER YOU'RE PANNING, TILTING, TRACKING OR ZOOMING NEVER, EVER CUT IN THE MIDDLE OF YOUR CAMERA MOVE. THIS JARS WITH AN AUDIENCE WORSE THAN NAILS BEING DRAGGED DOWN A BLACKBOARD.

A New Angle on Shots

There are basically three angles you can film from:

a) Low angles (where you look up at your subject)

b) Level with your subject

c) High angles (where you look down on your subject) - but of course, there are hundreds of variations between a) and c)!

You'll probably start off filming everything from eye level because that's what comes naturally - and because it's easier to hold and control the camera. Remember though that people sitting should be shot from their seated height and it's also far better to film children, babies and animals at their own level.

When you get more ambitious you can vary the angle to achieve different effects. Don't be afraid to experiment!

Low angles

Filming people from low down exaggerates height and implies importance, even dominance. (In film terms it's known as 'Subject strength/Viewer weakness' - bet you didn't know that!). You can make a

Beadle's 'Did You Know'

MOST PROFESSIONAL MOVIES ARE FILMED FROM CHEST HEIGHT BECAUSE IN THIS WAY THE AUDIENCE IS LOOKING UP AT THE STAR - IMPORTANT WHEN FILMING SOMEONE WITH THE STATURE (IN TERMS OF HEIGHT, NOT REPUTATION) OF SOMEONE LIKE TOM 'THUMB' CRUISE.

'baddie' look like a really nasty piece of work by crouching down as low as you can to film him.

Additionally, action looks more exciting when filmed from a low angle. A building shot from low down will also look much more dramatic. *Warning*: Your Auntie Jan might be very self-conscious of her double chin and huge, hirsute, canyon-like nostrils. Filming her from below will just accentuate these, leading to an unflattering shot and probably a clip round the ear.

High angles

Shooting people from above naturally has the opposite effect. It reduces their stature and suggests they are lonely, scared, insignificant, vulnerable - even weedy. Shooting action from a high angle isn't generally recommended; you'll find it lessens the drama and impact. However in comedy spy thrillers, this technique can be used effectively to imply that someone's being secretly observed.

Warning: Looking down on your subject might reveal too much of their thinning hair or a bald patch. Men in their thirties are particularly sensitive about this. Filming from above also makes your subject's eyes look narrower and might give the effect of someone squinting.

The Dutch Tilt

One of my favourite camera shots is the Dutch Tilt. Don't ask me why it's called the Dutch Tilt. It just is. It's easy to do - just hold your camcorder slightly on its side. You've seen the effect hundreds of times in action sequences; usually car chases in *The Professionals* or people running, where the tilt (often 45°) adds real drama and impact to the scene.

In comedy videos you can get laughs by applying the Dutch Tilt to objects you would never think as being fast and dramatic, such as an old lady walking, someone on a bicycle, someone riding a donkey, a child in a pedal car, a race between a Skoda and a Lada etc.

Buildings too, can be given the Dutch Tilt treatment so even the most mundane, everyday structure (for instance, a public library,

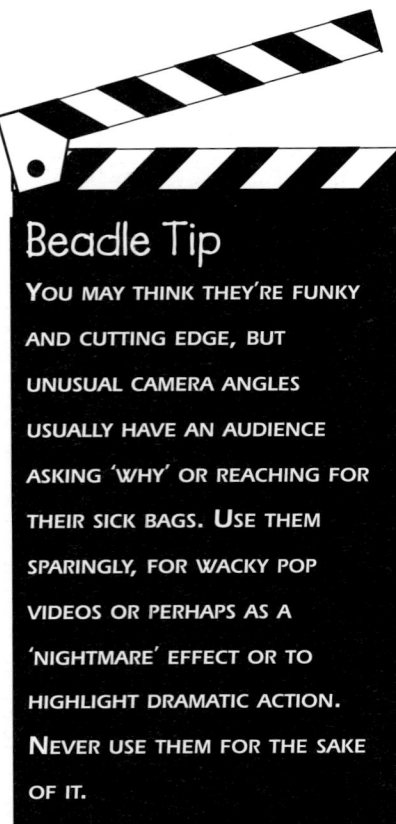

Beadle Tip

YOU MAY THINK THEY'RE FUNKY AND CUTTING EDGE, BUT UNUSUAL CAMERA ANGLES USUALLY HAVE AN AUDIENCE ASKING 'WHY' OR REACHING FOR THEIR SICK BAGS. USE THEM SPARINGLY, FOR WACKY POP VIDEOS OR PERHAPS AS A 'NIGHTMARE' EFFECT OR TO HIGHLIGHT DRAMATIC ACTION. NEVER USE THEM FOR THE SAKE OF IT.

outside lav, a chocolate box cottage etc.) can look dynamic or even foreboding.

It's best to make the tilt at least 30°. Any less and it can look like a mistake!

One last point, Dutch Tilts do not work effectively if the camera is hand held. Adopting this position with a tripod is easy. Just set your camcorder up as per normal - then make one of the tripod legs shorter than the others. Simple.

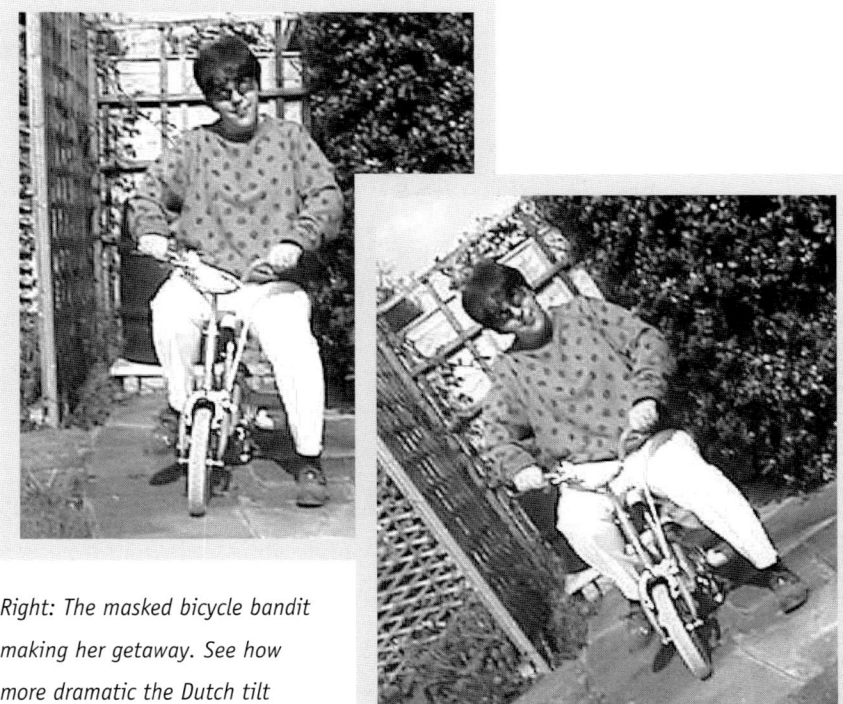

Right: The masked bicycle bandit making her getaway. See how more dramatic the Dutch tilt makes the second shot

Shooting From Cars - Some Useful Tips

★When filming from a car, let somebody else do the driving!

★I know I keep saying use a tripod, but shooting from a car is one of the rare occasions when you shouldn't. The reason is that vibration picked up from the road will travel up the tripod to your camcorder. It's far better to brace the camcorder securely against you, wedging yourself in position with pillows, a duvet or two or folded blankets, holding the camera very tightly to try and cushion any movement (don't get so snug that you fall asleep).

★Don't forget that you can film through the windscreen, any of the side windows or the back window. You may want to stand up and film through the sun roof. This is probably illegal and I didn't suggest it, OK.

★Drive slowly if you want to capture things close to you clearly.

★If filming through a windscreen you should switch your camera to manual and take a light reading from outside the vehicle.

★Likewise, check if your autofocus works when filming through the glass. A lot of cameras will focus on the window/windscreen itself, rather than the subject. If this is the case then you'll have to set a manual focus (setting your lens at its widest angle will increase the depth of field and help ensure that your subject stays sharp).

★Don't be tempted to film while standing on the roof of a moving vehicle, however adventurous this might seem.

Storyboards

Anyone planning to make a Blockbuster should use a storyboard. It's a sort of comic strip that breaks your video into a series of key shots with accompanying dialogue and directions. The good news is that you don't have to be able to draw to create a storyboard. Stick men are fine.

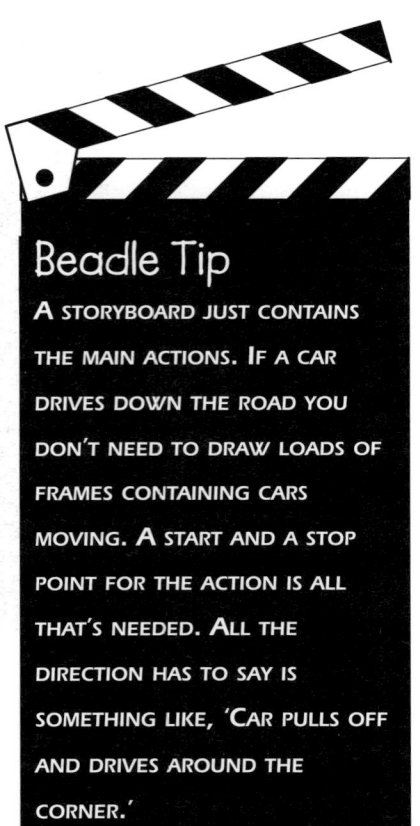

Advantages of a Storyboard

★A storyboard gives you, your performers and your crew an idea of what you're trying to achieve.

★If you're assembly editing (see p.130) then storyboards enable you to see at a glance which shots can be grouped together and filmed at the same time.

★A storyboard gives you an idea of what equipment or props you need for your shoot.

★It helps you keep a check on continuity. For example, if one of your cast is holding a briefcase in his left hand you can make a note on your storyboard to remind you of this. Similarly, if it's a shoot over a number of days you can record what people are wearing.

★It gives you time to develop your ideas and get them right rather than trying to wing it on the actual day of shooting. While drawing your storyboard you might think of a better way to film something – or you might decide that trying to recreate the Charge of the Light Brigade in your back garden is a tad too ambitious after all.

1. Four people sit nervously around a ouija board

Man 1: Is there anyone out there?

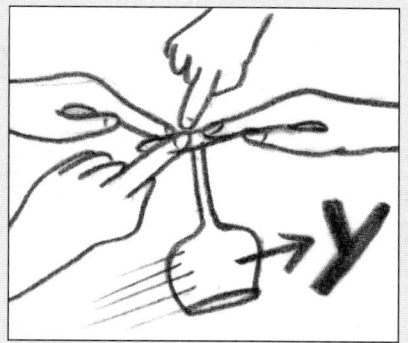

2. Suddenly the glass begins to move on to the letter 'Y'

Everyone gasps

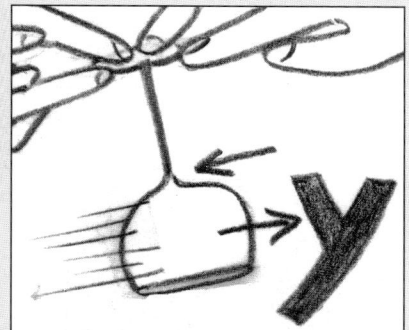

3. The glass continues to spell out 'Y'

Woman 1: Y...Y...Y...
Man 2: What can it mean?

4. The glass stops; everyone's confused

Woman 2: Oh my goodness! It's Uncle Eric!

5. The group look anxious

Man 2: (Nervously) How do you know?

6. Woman 2 faces the camera

Woman 2: Well, he had a terrible stutter!

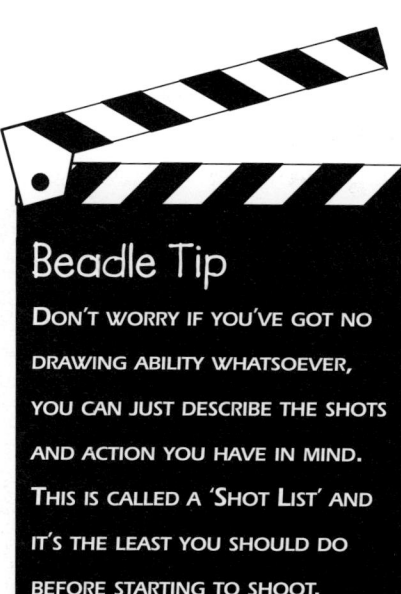

Beadle Tip

DON'T WORRY IF YOU'VE GOT NO DRAWING ABILITY WHATSOEVER, YOU CAN JUST DESCRIBE THE SHOTS AND ACTION YOU HAVE IN MIND. THIS IS CALLED A 'SHOT LIST' AND IT'S THE LEAST YOU SHOULD DO BEFORE STARTING TO SHOOT.

Casting Pearls Before Swine . . .

You should be thinking about casting even as you're creating ideas for your Blockbuster. If you don't know any musclemen, then your muscleman identity parade sketch is a non-starter. If however your Uncle Billy (or Auntie Gertrude) is a dead ringer for Christopher Lee, it would be a shame not to do a Dracula spoof.

So, who's going to be in your Blockbuster? Who can you ask? At first the choice may seem pretty limited, but you probably know more people than you think.

Looks Like Typecasting to Me

'Typage' is when you cast someone according to their looks. For example, if you had a mate who was six foot five with insanely piercing eyes and long wild black hair, he'd be first choice for the part of Rasputin in your sketch. If you had a nephew with two heads, he'd be great to play the mutant in your sci-fi epic, and so on.

Audiences expect characters to look a certain way, which is why you cast your wife or girlfriend as the pretty heroine and your granny as the evil witch, and not the other way around.

That's not to say, of course, that you can't cast against type for extra comedy effect. So your grandad weighs seven and a half stone, is five foot one, bald as a coot and wears thick spectacles and a hearing aid. Who better to play Ben Hur in your spoof!

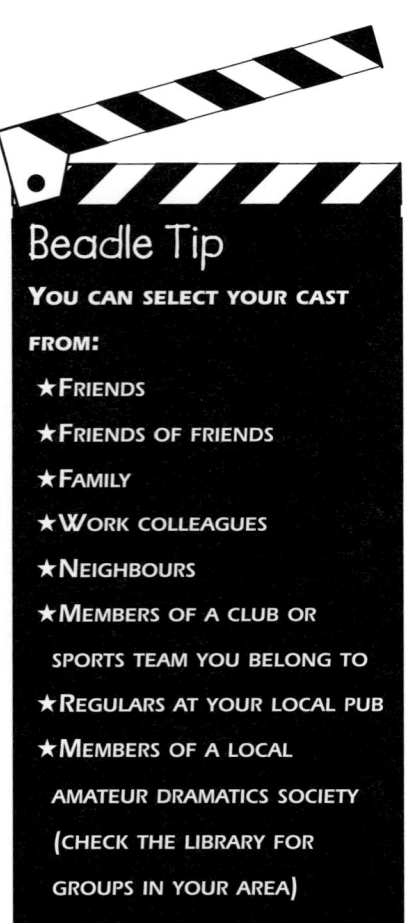

Beadle Tip

YOU CAN SELECT YOUR CAST FROM:

★ FRIENDS

★ FRIENDS OF FRIENDS

★ FAMILY

★ WORK COLLEAGUES

★ NEIGHBOURS

★ MEMBERS OF A CLUB OR SPORTS TEAM YOU BELONG TO

★ REGULARS AT YOUR LOCAL PUB

★ MEMBERS OF A LOCAL AMATEUR DRAMATICS SOCIETY (CHECK THE LIBRARY FOR GROUPS IN YOUR AREA)

Casting Against Type

Mad Glaswegians	make great	Roman Emperors
Frail grannies	make great	Mafia bosses
Little kids	make great	World-weary cynics
Overweight men	make great	Action heroes
Elderly gentlemen	make great	Casanovas
Amateur boxers	make great	Transvestites

Approaching Prospective Cast Members

★ Ask your prospective cast members straight out if they'd like to take part. Don't beat about the bush or try to get them in a situation where they can't say no. Inevitably, you will get a rejection or two. Some people would rather die than stand in front of a camera. That's just the way they are – but you'll be surprised how many will also say yes, including the most unlikely of people in some cases.

★ Making a Blockbuster can be great fun – but it can also be hard work. Make sure people know what they're letting themselves in for.

★ Have your rehearsal and shooting schedule and location ideas worked out in advance. Be able to tell your cast where and when they'll be needed – and for how long. That way, they're less likely to let you down.

★ Let them see a script or storyboard as soon as possible – and never hide things from your cast members. No one wants to turn up for shooting only to be told, 'I forgot to mention – this scene requires you to fall into an open cesspit and be entirely submerged!' You may find yourself minus one thespian!

★ Offer reassurance. Some people would sincerely like to take part but may feel nervous about their abilities. Assure them it will be fun and that everyone taking part is just as amateur. Tell them it's not the end of the world if they mess something up.

BE POLITE. HERE'S HOW NOT TO APPROACH FRIENDS AND FAMILY WITH YOUR CASTING IDEAS:

★ 'I CAN'T AFFORD MUCH MAKE-UP, SO I THOUGHT YOU'D BE GREAT AS FRANKENSTEIN'S MONSTER.'

★ 'YOU LOOK STUPID, SO I THOUGHT YOU COULD PLAY THE VILLAGE IDIOT.'

★ 'YOU'VE GOT THE KIND OF GRATING VOICE THIS PART IS CRYING OUT FOR.'

★ 'YOU LOOK MUCH OLDER THAN YOU ARE, SO YOU BE THE GRANDMOTHER.'

★ 'I WROTE THIS PART FOR YOU; IT'S A BALDING MAN IN HIS FIFTIES WHO LOOKS LIKE HE MIGHT SMELL.'

★ Don't try to pester or blackmail reluctant people into taking part. Their heart won't be in the project.

★ Make everything fun for your cast and crew. If they have fun taking part, they'll take a greater pride in it.

Hidden Talents

Many of the people around you may have talents you never suspected. Some people can do the most amazing things. Try to find out if anyone in your potential cast has a hidden talent you can make use of. What sort of 'hidden talents' do I mean? Perhaps something like: juggling, piano playing, singing, snooker, disco dancing, burping the National Anthem or riding a unicycle underwater.

Make use of these things – but make sure they're relevant. If your Uncle Dave is a keen yodeller, then build the sketch around his dubious skill. It could be about a yodelling cowboy or perhaps we're in the future, where 'Big Brother' rules supreme and yodelling is outlawed.

Use your cast's hidden talents well and it'll bring the house down at your premiere!

Of course, a hidden skill can also be something intangible – like natural comic timing.

Hiring and Firing – Don't!

There's nothing worse than giving someone a big part in your Blockbuster, getting them to change their plans to suit you, making them excited about the project – and then finding that they're the most hopeless actor on earth. Are you really going to fire grandad who's postponed his chest X-ray so that he can be on set with you all day?

Before you promise anyone anything, get an idea of what they can do. Show them the script on the pretext of asking their opinions and their help. Ideally get them to read a couple of the parts and get a feel for what they can achieve before you cast them.

Simply the Best!

They say never work with children or animals.

Wrong!

Kids and pets look great up on screen, and they never fail to get the biggest laughs. With a cute toddler or a dopey looking dog, you've got the audience in the palm of your hand right from the start.

Children

Most kids are natural hams and will love to be part of your production.

You cast them alongside adults in a 'mixed' production but – be warned now – they're going to steal the show! So play to that, let the kids come out on top in your sketch. If you're doing something like *Oliver Twist,* for example, make sure you end on a big finish where Oliver triumphs and the grown-ups are thoroughly humiliated.

Alternatively, you can work with an all-child cast. Maybe it's a take-off of *Grange Hill.* If you're old enough to remember them, it could be a spoof of *The Famous Five* (and you get a dog thrown in for extra cuteness!). 'Five Go to Newport Pagnell' anyone? It could be the story of some kids who want to form their own pop group. Maybe it's *Village of the Damned* 1998-style. Or how about a home-grown video talent show where kids can sing and dance, do impressions, tell jokes, play musical instruments – and shine!

Remember, there's a *lot* of fun to be had from kids acting or pretending to be grown up. Perhaps your sketch features three adult characters. Now imagine three kids playing the parts. Would it be more fun? Perhaps you should consider it.

The wider the age discrepancy the better. Kids playing at grandparents can be enormous fun or, to go to the other extreme, take the next approach, for example:

Sweeney Toddlers

Have you ever thought about remaking *The Sweeney* with a couple of toddlers? No? I'm not surprised really, but it's perfectly possible and should be very funny.

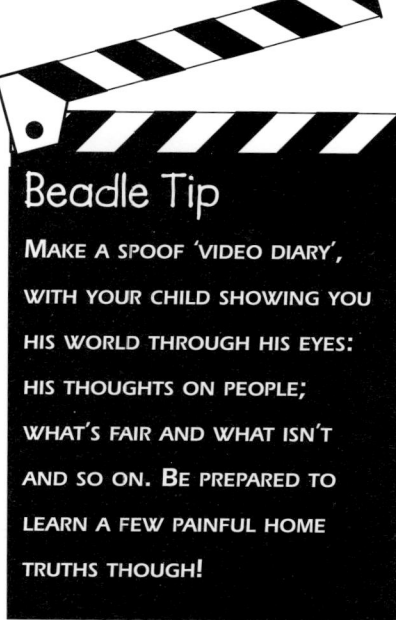

Beadle Tip

MAKE A SPOOF 'VIDEO DIARY', WITH YOUR CHILD SHOWING YOU HIS WORLD THROUGH HIS EYES: HIS THOUGHTS ON PEOPLE; WHAT'S FAIR AND WHAT ISN'T AND SO ON. BE PREPARED TO LEARN A FEW PAINFUL HOME TRUTHS THOUGH!

The Sweeney Toddlers

We're the Sweeney son – and we ain't had our dinner!

Of course, to really work, you'd want to use the original voices off a *Sweeney* episode so that little Daniel sounds like John Thaw and tiny Nathan sounds like Dennis Waterman. (Oh yes, there's that little matter of copyright again. Naturally, I can't condone this sort of outrageous behaviour, so it's up to you.) Take a chase scene. You'd film your toddlers running down the street and use the original soundtrack played over this action: 'Head him off rahnd the back, George!' little Daniel bellows as he toddles furiously. 'Right ho, guvnor!' tiny Nathan seems to reply. You get the gist . . .

Of course, you can do this with any TV show, past or present. It doesn't have to be *The Sweeney*. That was just an excuse for me to make a terrible pun at the start.

Filming child stars – some tips

★Shoot some point-of-view shots from the height of your child actors so that your audience can see the world through their eyes.

★Remember that children have a short attention span and get bored easily. Make everything as much fun as possible and don't lose your patience.

★Above all, put safety first. Never get so carried away when you're making your Blockbuster that you subject your child stars to the slightest danger. Think before every shot, and make sure there's a 'child wrangler' on hand to scoop up the little darlings if they suddenly decide to run off or do anything daft.

Dogs

Dogs are great. Stupid, but great. Most know at least how to 'sit', 'come', 'bark', 'catch' or 'lie down' on cue, which is more than most human actors can accomplish. And that's all you need. Well, that and a few tit-bits as bribes!

A scene from Four Weddings and a Kennel

Dogs are probably the easiest animals to fit into your Blockbuster. Build their actions and their movements around what you know they can do – especially any little tricks.

Maybe your poodle can be a bloodhound in that spoof on *The Fugitive* you're planning, or the Colditz prison guard dog. Of course, you could always base your whole show around the dog. What about a *Lassie* spoof. Maybe it's about a doggie detective – Sherlock Bones . . .

If you've got a dog and there's a chance to use it somehow, do. With a dog, the possibilities are endless. And you thought it was just a good-for-nothing fleabag!

Cats

Ever tried to get a cat to do anything? It's impossible. When you want them to sit still, they move. When you want them to move, they decide it's time to curl up and have forty winks (or a thousand and forty if your cat's anything like mine).

The solution is to take a leaf from director Mike Leigh's book. Let your cat improvise. Film it doing whatever it is it likes to do. Mix your shots and be sure to take some close-ups of the cat's face.

Now it's time for 'Cat-Cam'! Get down on your knees and elbows and film the cat's point-of-view as it walks across the room or nuzzles into its food bowl. Film people in the house from right down on the

Stinky, the cat that ate Peterborough

floor, as if the cat were looking up at them. Film things that the cat is sure to be interested in, like fish swimming around their tank.

After you've got your shots, you can start to assemble your story. Maybe it's a day in the life of your cat. Maybe it's 'The thoughts of Chairman Kitty' with someone doing the 'voice' of your cat, commenting on the dreadful humans it's forced to share space with. You can do more with your cat than you think!

Your Technical Crew

People who may not want to be in front of the camera are sometimes perfectly happy to serve behind it. If someone's turned you down for a part, they may still want to be a member of the technical crew.

Crew?

Of course, you could always try to handle every technical aspect of the shoot yourself – but you'd be far better off with a few helping hands to cover sound, lighting and so on, saving you precious time and allowing you to concentrate on directing.

When a big TV comedy sketch show goes out on location, there are probably close to fifty or sixty people involved. There are mobile catering vans, huge trucks for equipment, coaches for the crew and trailers for the stars.

You'll probably have to make do with three or four mates crammed into someone's Ford Escort.

This then, will be your crew. But

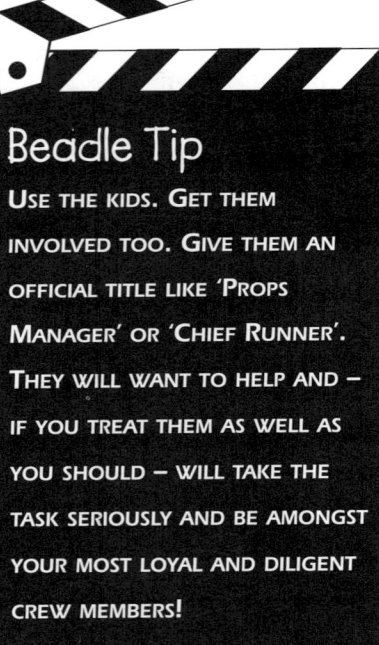

Beadle Tip

USE THE KIDS. GET THEM INVOLVED TOO. GIVE THEM AN OFFICIAL TITLE LIKE 'PROPS MANAGER' OR 'CHIEF RUNNER'. THEY WILL WANT TO HELP AND – IF YOU TREAT THEM AS WELL AS YOU SHOULD – WILL TAKE THE TASK SERIOUSLY AND BE AMONGST YOUR MOST LOYAL AND DILIGENT CREW MEMBERS!

what do they all do, apart from eat all the sandwiches and come up with funnier jokes than you've got in your script?

Camera operator (maybe you)

The person who films the action, following your storyboard. An ability to lug an unbelievably heavy tripod around is a bonus.

Sound person

In charge of positioning the microphone(s) to get the best results and generally ensuring good sound quality. A keen sense of hearing is desirable.

Lighting person

Has to make sure each scene is lit properly, but is also responsible for the uncreative (but still vital) task of changing bulbs and making sure no one trips over cables.

The personal assistant

Logs the shots, notes any script changes or changes to shots, keeps an eye on continuity, dishes out the sandwiches and smoothes out bad feelings on the set when you keep shouting at everyone. Great job.

The problem is that your technical crew is not likely to be very technical – at least to start with. If you've read this book cover to cover, you'll know far more about their jobs than they will. Help them out, explain what's needed of them, lend them this book or – better still – buy them each a copy.

Sound and lighting in particular are quite complex and will benefit from being handled by a person with a technical mind. Do you know someone who can programme their own VCR? Or who can take one look under your bonnet and say, 'Oh yeah, I see the problem – it's your induction coil manifold, mate'? That's the person you're ideally looking for!

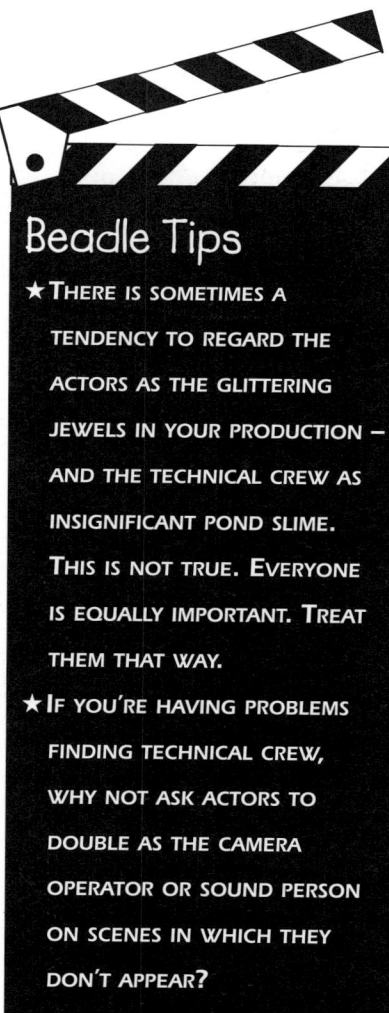

Beadle Tips

★ THERE IS SOMETIMES A TENDENCY TO REGARD THE ACTORS AS THE GLITTERING JEWELS IN YOUR PRODUCTION – AND THE TECHNICAL CREW AS INSIGNIFICANT POND SLIME. THIS IS NOT TRUE. EVERYONE IS EQUALLY IMPORTANT. TREAT THEM THAT WAY.

★ IF YOU'RE HAVING PROBLEMS FINDING TECHNICAL CREW, WHY NOT ASK ACTORS TO DOUBLE AS THE CAMERA OPERATOR OR SOUND PERSON ON SCENES IN WHICH THEY DON'T APPEAR?

Locations

FILMING AND THE POLICE

IF YOU ARE MAKING A BLOCKBUSTER ON PUBLIC PROPERTY IT'S USEFUL TO ALERT THE LOCAL POLICE. THEIR CONCERN WILL BE THAT YOU HAVE THE NECESSARY PERMISSIONS, THAT YOU'RE NOT TRESPASSING OR CAUSING A NUISANCE OR AN OBSTRUCTION. HOWEVER, THEY DO TAKE A VERY DIM VIEW OF PEOPLE FILMING BANKS, BUILDING SOCIETIES — ANYWHERE LARGE AMOUNTS OF MONEY ARE STORED. FOR ALL THEY KNOW YOU MIGHT BE 'CASING THE JOINT'. ADDITIONALLY, THEY DON'T APPROVE OF POLICE STATIONS BEING FILMED.

The next thing you need to consider is where you are going to film your Blockbuster. You may decide you can film it all in one place, or that you need several different locations to tell your story.

It's a good idea to be thinking about locations even as you're writing. Using what's around you simplifies things greatly. Use the park, the pub, the shops, the car park, the alleyway, the garden and so on.

If you have access to a particularly interesting location then seriously consider using it. For example, maybe you work as a sewage engineer and you have access to miles of mysterious Victorian tunnels. Great! Use it – and best of luck finding a cast and crew! Maybe at work there's a vast warehouse which would be just the place for a criminal gang to plot their dire deeds . . .

Once you've decided on the location or locations you want to use, it's time to check them out to make sure they're as suitable as you think they are . . .

The Recce

One of the skills you need as a video maker is being able to assess the suitability of locations for shooting. Professionals call this doing a 'recce' (short for 'reconnaissance').

Take 'rough' shots with your

camcorder as well as still photographs – these will be useful for showing to your cast/crew in advance, and for working out the best angles to shoot from and whether you'll encounter any practical problems with filming. (For this reason it's always best to take your crew with you.)

If possible, do your recce on the same day of the week and at the same time of the day you intend to shoot. That way, you won't recce an empty field on Tuesday only to discover that, on Saturdays, the location always plays host to the largest gathering of Euro-juggernauts in Britain.

A Recce Checklist

★Which angles are best to film from?

★Note the position of the sun and the difference in shadows cast: a doorway that's brightly lit at 11am might be in gloom by 3pm.

★Is there somewhere to park - and can you be sure of getting a space?

★If you're planning to run your camera off the car battery, can you get your car close enough without driving across those immaculate lawns with the 'Keep off the grass' signs dotted all over them?

★Where will you shelter if it starts to rain?

★Where's the nearest telephone box - in case someone doesn't show up or there's an emergency?

★Is there somewhere for the cast to sit and rest in between takes?

★Will there be anything in shot that shouldn't really be there? (e.g. someone plotting to take over the world would probably not have his HQ adjacent to a children's playground, a wholesaler of orthopaedic shoes – or a police station).

★If you're filming somewhere like a park, check to make sure nothing else is planned on the day of shooting. You don't want to turn up only to find the 'World Shouting Championships' or the '2000 Years of Fireworks Celebrations' are being held in the same location!

★Is there a busy road running right in front of the location that will prevent you getting clear shots of it?

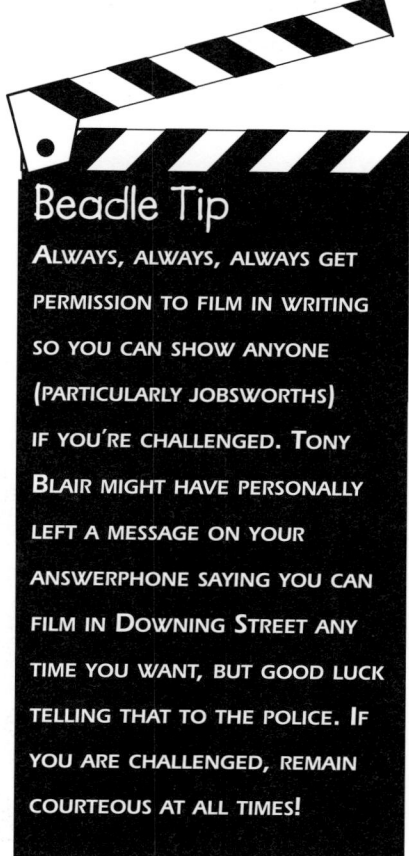

Beadle Tip

ALWAYS, ALWAYS, ALWAYS GET PERMISSION TO FILM IN WRITING SO YOU CAN SHOW ANYONE (PARTICULARLY JOBSWORTHS) IF YOU'RE CHALLENGED. TONY BLAIR MIGHT HAVE PERSONALLY LEFT A MESSAGE ON YOUR ANSWERPHONE SAYING YOU CAN FILM IN DOWNING STREET ANY TIME YOU WANT, BUT GOOD LUCK TELLING THAT TO THE POLICE. IF YOU ARE CHALLENGED, REMAIN COURTEOUS AT ALL TIMES!

★ Do you need mains power for lights? If so, where are the nearest sockets?

★ Do you need permission to film at the location or are there any restrictions (i.e. some locations won't allow the use of tripods)?

★ Is there a pub or somewhere to eat close by if you're not planning a packed lunch?

Weather

There's a reason this book was launched in the summer. Good weather is very important to location filming. A grey, overcast day, as you'd expect, appears subdued on video. Detail is lost. Despite what manufacturers tell you, camcorders really like as much light as possible. If you can, film out on location when the weather's good and do your interiors when it's not. Be prepared enough to change your plans around at the last minute.

Never film in rain unless you can absolutely 100 per cent shelter your camera – not just the lens but the whole camera. Camcorders are remarkably unwaterproof and you could end up with a very expensive repair bill. Don't forget your cast and crew. They might not be expecting Oscars, but they're not expecting pneumonia either.

High winds are another very real problem, so avoid exposed places if you don't want your location to sound like a desolate, windswept moor. On some camcorders, even the slightest breeze can sound like Hurricane Sharon over the microphone.

Settled snow can look very dramatic on camera, but sunlight reflecting off it can play havoc with the shot, leading to that smeared, burned out effect on your tape. You may need a polarising filter to take the heat off it.

Catering

If you're expecting people to be working out on location for several hours, it's only polite to have some snack food to hand. Be especially sure to bring along plenty to drink. This is not to keep Cousin Wayne happy and stop him getting the shakes. A thirsty cast and crew is a ratty cast and crew. If they start getting tired and parched, there's a chance they'll abandon your location for the pub!

The Joy of Sets

Your home contains a wealth of ready-made sets. You've got a kitchen for those cookery sketches and those advertising parodies. There's a master bedroom for those farces and 'love interest' videos. There's a bathroom for the *Psycho* parody and the Cadbury's Flake ad. A dining room for those witty dinner party pieces and a lounge for your sit-coms and where your detective can reveal just who murdered the butler – and why . . .

You may have a shed for those DIY programme spoofs and a garden for your *Gardener's World* parody. What you don't realise, however, is that your home contains far more versatile sets than you realise.

There's a Teleportation Pod in Your Bathroom – and You Didn't Even Know It!

OK, it might look like a shower enclosure at the moment but with a little imagination, some old TV parts and a few pieces of metallic card, your bathroom could be

TELEPORTATION POD

transformed into the sort of place where you'd carry out matter transference. The key to making any set work is to improvise. So what if you don't have a shower enclosure? Instead, what about a large cardboard box – the type washing machines come in – painted silver. Even a wardrobe or a broom cupboard with the sign 'Teleportation Pod' on it will do. No one will really believe it's a teleportation pod but that doesn't matter. It's all part of the fun.

Beadle Tips

★ DON'T LET YOUR SET LOOK TOO CLUTTERED. TRY AND MAKE THE BACKGROUNDS AS UNCOMPLICATED AS POSSIBLE.

★ FOR THE SAME REASON, AVOID ANY WALLS OR CURTAINS THAT HAVE HEAVY CHEQUERED OR DIAGONAL PATTERNS. THESE ARE VERY DISTRACTING AND CAN CAUSE WHAT'S KNOWN AS 'STROBING'. IN THIS CASE YOUR AUDIENCE WILL EITHER BE ADJUSTING THEIR EYES – OR THEIR TV SET.

★ MAKE SURE YOUR ACTORS HAVE ENOUGH ROOM TO WALK AROUND WITHOUT TRIPPING OVER CABLES, PROPS OR EACH OTHER.

★ LIGHT WILL TEND TO FLARE OFF VERY SHINY OBJECTS IN SHOT (IF THESE ARE NECESSARY, USE A DULLING SPRAY – AVAILABLE FROM ART AND CRAFT SHOPS – TO LESSEN THE EFFECT).

How to Transform Your Lounge into the Bridge of a Starship

 MOUNT TWO FOLDED UMBRELLAS ON THE WALL LIKE CROSSED SWORDS TO REPRESENT THE SYMBOL OF THE INTERGALACTIC SPACE FEDERATION.

TO SIMULATE THE SPACESHIP'S HALF-ALIEN FIRST OFFICER, DRESS A FRIEND UP IN A TOGA AND SELLOTAPE A BATTERY POWERED SMOKE ALARM TO HER FOREHEAD. HAVE HER STAND FAITHFULLY AND EMOTIONLESSLY AT HER CAPTAIN'S SIDE.

CLEAR ONE WALL OF THE ROOM. NEXT, COVER IT WITH BACO FOIL FROM CARPET TO CEILING TO GIVE A HI-TECH METALLIC LOOK.

REPLACE THE NORMAL LIGHT BULBS WITH RED ONES TO GIVE AN UNEARTHLY GLOW TO THE STARSHIP BRIDGE (AND TO HELP DISGUISE THE SWIRLY UPHOLSTERY).

POSITION A LAVA LAMP ON EACH END OF THE ARMCHAIR BACK. THEY MAKE GREAT ANTI-MATTER CONTAINMENT PODS. TRUST ME.

POSITION AN ARMCHAIR FACING AWAY FROM THE WALL. THIS IS THE CAPTAIN'S COMMAND SEAT.

SELLOTAPE STRIPS OF WORKING CHRISTMAS LIGHTS ALONG THE ARMS OF THE ARMCHAIR TO SIMULATE COMMAND WARNING LIGHTS.

WHEN THE SHIP GOES INTO HYPERDRIVE, SIMULATE THE SOUND BY TURNING ON YOUR VACUUM CLEANER AND GETTING THE CREW TO SWAY FROM SIDE TO SIDE.

STICK A PICTURE OF MR SPOCK TO THE INSIDE OF THE MICROWAVE DOOR TO SIMULATE THE CAPTAIN'S PERSONAL DEEP SPACE VIDEO COMMUNICATOR IN ACTION. (WHOEVER PLAYS THE CAPTAIN MUST TRY TO TALK TO THE MICROWAVE WITHOUT LAUGHING.)

PUT AN OCCASIONAL TABLE TO ONE SIDE OF THE ARMCHAIR AND PLACE YOUR MICROWAVE OVEN ON IT.

Above: Captain Mary and half-alien first officer Philippa stand fearless in the face of impending Klingon attack

Garages

A film set is just a large empty expanse under cover – which is also what a garage is. OK, it might not be that roomy at the moment, but clear out those garden chairs, the hamster cage (for goodness' sake, he's been dead for twelve years and there's only so long you can mourn), the bikes, the unused exercise equipment and that old cooker, and the garage becomes, in effect, your studio. Without carpets, furniture, wallpaper or fragile ornaments to worry about, you can dress a garage in any way you like, although bare breeze block or brick walls make a good prison cell, interrogation room or torture chamber.

The Dining Room

Your dining room can be transformed into an office, an operating theatre, Frankenstein's lab, a mortuary or a black magic altar simply by decorating and adding appropriate props to the dining room table. As long as it's rectangular, that is. Of course, if it's circular you're well placed for that King Arthur sketch.

The Garden

Moving your camera through thick foliage as you film can give the impression that you're in a jungle. With control panels, switches and instrumentation strategically placed, conservatories and greenhouses can be used to re-create the glass cockpits of World War Two bombers (if possible, use your camcorder's Automatic Backlight Control to compensate for the brightness of the sky behind your actors).

Lofts

Believe it or not, the highest room in the house is useful for creating the impression of an underground chamber, a dungeon, a cellar or a secret subterranean hideout. Light the loft dimly, keeping large areas in shadow. If there's a skylight, try filming your Blockbuster illuminated only by natural light – after first masking the windows so that only a square foot of glass is visible. This can give a good impression of light entering from ground level and

CHANGING SKYLINES

IF YOU'RE FILMING INSIDE BUT WANT TO GIVE THE IMPRESSION THAT YOU'RE IN A MUCH MORE EXOTIC LOCATION THEN PAINT A NEW SKYLINE ON A LARGE PIECE OF CARD OR HARDBOARD AND POSITION THIS A FEW FEET OUTSIDE A GROUND FLOOR WINDOW. DEPENDING ON YOUR ARTISTIC SKILLS THIS COULD SHOW MANHATTAN SKYSCRAPERS, A MARTIAN LANDSCAPE, SNOW-COVERED MOUNTAINS, DEEP SPACE, EVEN TELETUBBY LAND. WHEN FILMING, BE CAREFUL SHADOWS DON'T FALL ON THIS PAINTED SCENERY AND REMEMBER TO PROP THE ROOM IN SYMPATHY WITH THE EXTERIOR YOU'RE TRYING TO RE-CREATE (FOR INSTANCE, IF YOU'RE TRYING TO RE-CREATE A WALL STREET OFFICE THEN TAKE THOSE FLYING DUCKS DOWN).

VERY IMPORTANT WARNING!!!

THE FLOORING IN LOFTS IS VERY, VERY FRAGILE. UNLESS YOU REALLY WANT TO POKE YOUR FOOT THROUGH A TOP FLOOR CEILING, ONLY WALK ON THE JOISTS OR, BETTER STILL, WHERE THESE HAVE BEEN BOARDED OVER.

shining down on a basement.

You can disguise the slope of the roof, rafters, water tanks and pipes by covering them with old sheets, painted to resemble stone, as if the room you're in has been hewn from solid rock.

Cars

Because they have seats, a steering wheel, instruments and are quite compact, cars are good for recreating the cockpit of some sort of craft. It could be a jet fighter, a one-man submarine, a space ship or an armoured fighting vehicle. Oh yes. They're also extremely useful for sketches involving motor cars.

Your performer sits in the driver's seat while you film through the open passenger's door or through the windscreen. The first thing to do, though, is to change the scenery visible through the car windows (it can be quite difficult keeping up the

Brave Captain Barney prepares to engage the Xirgon Battle Fleet in his StarWing Fighter (formerly a Fiat Punto)

pretence that you're 500 feet below the Atlantic Ocean when your neighbour walks past the window with her poodle).

You can paint a new background on what's known as a 'flat' – basically a large piece of hardboard or canvas stretched over a frame.

74

Alternatively, paint scenery on the back of an old wallpaper roll. If you get two friends to unroll it as you film, this will give the impression that your craft is moving. Another way to give this effect is by getting someone holding a plant or large shrub to crawl or walk past below the car window, then duck back and do the same again and again – all the while staying well out of shot. (If you do this, make sure the plant is held at different heights each time so it doesn't look like it's the same one.)

When filming, go for a tight shot to disguise the fact that you're in an Austin Montego rather than an F-117 stealth bomber. All you should ideally see is the 'pilot' and the instrumentation of some sort. OK, I know a steering wheel doesn't look like an aircraft joystick but you can always get round that by getting your actor to sit in the front *passenger* seat, holding a computer games joystick as some sort of control mechanism.

You can supplement controls/switches etc. by painting dials, levers, gauges, buttons etc. on card to cover up the inside of the doors (attach these with self-adhesive velcro).

Cardboard Boxes

Joining several large cardboard boxes together after removing the tops and bottoms can create a convincing-looking tunnel or shaft. Again, film close in so all you see is the interior of the tunnel – and your actor climbing through it. Tilting your camcorder at an angle while you film will heighten suspense, particularly if you're trying to give the impression of someone being chased through the tunnel.

You might only have a run of, say, ten feet of boxes but cutting several shots together – using different angles – will give the impression that the tunnel goes on for miles. Perhaps it's an air conditioning shaft in the HQ of an evil mastermind, or ducting running through a nuclear power plant. Inter-cutting these shots with a shot of an air vent in a wall will add to the impression that someone is really in the shaft.

Children's play tunnels can also be used in the same way. These are normally translucent which means you can get some interesting effects by illuminating them from the outside.

OTHER WAYS TO MAKE IT LOOK LIKE YOU'RE ACTUALLY MOVING:

★ GET SOMEONE TO ROCK THE CAR GENTLY FROM SIDE TO SIDE.

★ ROCKING IT MORE VIOLENTLY WILL SIMULATE TURBULENCE AS IF IN A PLANE (ADDING DEEP, BASS SOUNDS LIKE THE LOW RUMBLE OF AN ENGINE WILL ALSO HELP THE EFFECT). REMEMBER, HOLDING YOUR CAMCORDER AT AN ANGLE WILL LOOK LIKE THE CRAFT IS CLIMBING, OR DIVING.

★ IF YOU'RE FILMING WHEN IT'S APPROACHING DUSK, GET AN ASSISTANT TO SHINE A TORCH ACROSS YOUR ACTOR'S FACE TO SIMULATE LIGHTS MOVING PAST.

Exotic Sets and Locations – The Art of Illusion

If your video Blockbuster is set in modern times and in everyday life, then chances are all the locations and sets you need are at home or just around the corner.

If, on the other hand, your Blockbuster is set in some foreign place and time, you'll need to create an illusion. Say, for example, your Blockbuster is set in Ancient Rome. It would be wonderful if you could build a replica of the Coliseum, and get a few charioteers in to ride about in the background. But you can't. So what do you do? You create a shorthand version of Rome instead. You dress your actors in togas, shoot in a neutral, nondescript location that passes for Ancient Rome and – hey presto – your audience is transported.

Audiences love to jump to assumptions – and they'll do most of the work for you!

What techniques can you use?

Cheat by Using Establishing Shots

What do I mean by this? Well, suppose you're making your own version of *Prisoner Cell Block H*. You might use bunk beds in a corner of an empty bedroom to simulate a prison cell (actually, I think the real series did this), but the way to make this set look more authentic is to start your video with an exterior shot of a *real prison*. This is what's known as your 'establishing shot'. It tells your audience where the video takes place, when it takes place, and gives an idea of what's going to happen.

If you don't live near a real prison then improvise. What about filming a close-up of an iron grille over a window, followed by filming keys being inserted into various locks? Or shoot an old factory or warehouse with sounds of cell doors being slammed shut, and then use a brief close-up of a home-made sign that says something like: *'H M Prison, Wormwood Scrubs. Keep in'*.

This principle applies anywhere your video is supposed to take place – a hospital, a coal mine, the space shuttle, a castle, The Bank of England, on board the *Titanic*, halfway up Mont Blanc, all the way up Mont Blanc etc. By using establishing shots in this way, you're letting the audience 'write the show' in their minds. Give them a simple visual (or sound) clue and their imagination will do the rest.

Other sources of establishing shots

★Your own holiday videos – e.g. shots of airports, beaches, hotels, stately homes, art galleries, museums, historic monuments etc.

★Clips taped from the news or films. For example, for a horror movie spoof, you might use clips of Frankenstein's Castle from a real old horror film. That way you could get the use of a $150,000 set for nothing – which must be a bargain. I'm not condoning this – or even suggesting you do it – but this practice has been known to take place . . .

★Similarly, it is possible (but again, I wouldn't want to suggest it) to video photographs from books, newspapers etc. (Strictly speaking, even though you'll be using these for home use only, you still need to obtain the photograph copyright holder's permission to use them – but I won't tell if you don't.)

★Toys: use model soldiers, castles, cars, aircraft etc. to set the scene – remember it is a comedy video you're making. (The same thing applies to props in general, e.g. using some simple Halloween gimmicks to establish something like a witches' coven.)

★People dressed in period costume.

★Animals: extreme close-ups of creatures will set the scene for something like 'Invasion of the Giant Earthworm' or 'The Chihuahua That Ate Cardiff'. In these cases, don't stand at a distance and zoom in to the creature; get really close – as close as you can – and use a wide angle. This will make the creature really fill your viewfinder and distort its features so it looks creepy and menacing.

Everything in its Place

After you've used your 'cheat' establishing scene to tell your audience where they are, you still have to work to maintain the illusion. You can't flash up a picture of Monte Carlo and then cut to a shot of what is very obviously Fulham High Street (well, you can, and it might actually be very funny, but it depends on whether you want to make a joke of playing with your audience's expectations).

The real locations you use will somehow have to look like the exotic locations they're meant to be. This may mean using very bland, non-specific locations with little scenery. However, it's more fun to spend a little time and think about how you can further improve on your illusion.

For example, how can you physically create a desert scene? The beach, especially if it has sand dunes, is an obvious choice of location, but it may not be feasible to get there. So maybe there's a pile of sand in a local builder's yard or construction site. Two hands claw their way over the top of the heap. A wretched, reddened face gasps, 'Water! Water!' and you're suddenly in the desert. If you're shooting tight enough, you can use a long-jump pit in a sports ground, or even a child's sand pit. You can put a few tall rubber plants around a child's paddling pool – and you've got an oasis.

What else do you associate with the desert? Heat. So have a 'hot' filter on your video, make your actors look sweat drenched and dehydrated and have them swat at imaginary flies. Vaseline is great for creating that all over sweaty skin look.

Sound Thinking

I've always loved radio – because the pictures are better! The sounds you hear on radio create pictures in your head – and *you* can use sound to help bring your locations to life as well.

When you're trying to re-create some exotic locale, don't just think about what it looks like. Think what it sounds like too.

You can use sound to transport your viewers almost anywhere. Dub on the sound of seagulls and suddenly you're in a harbour. Dub on shouts, explosions and gunfire and your audience is in the middle of a fierce battle. They may not actually see the sea, or the soldiers fighting up there on the screen, but inside their heads their brains are putting it all together for you.

You can use music in the same way. Play something oriental and your audience 'knows' they're looking at Japan or China. Play some oom-pa-pa and they see the Austrian Tyrol (and someone with an appalling record collection).

You Are Wear You Are!

Costumes give a good sense of location too. When an audience sees a toga, they automatically assume they're in the ancient world – unless of course, your character is sitting in Spud-U-Like, in which case they assume they're looking at a nutter! Provided you don't spoil their sense of location by throwing in an anachronism, such as a car or a parade of shops, you've successfully transported them!

Cowboy costumes mean the Wild West. A white roll-neck pullover, a black peak cap and a pair of binoculars put you on the bridge of a World War Two destroyer. A beret, a stripy jumper and a string of onions say France.

Zis is zer city of luv!

OTHER TRICKS

WE TALKED A MOMENT AGO ABOUT BEING ON THE BRIDGE OF A WORLD WAR TWO DESTROYER. HOW ELSE CAN YOU SUPPORT THE ILLUSION? THE SOUND OF WAVES CRASHING IS ONE THING. GETTING YOUR PERFORMERS TO SWAY SLIGHTLY OR STAGGER HELPS, AS DOES MOVING THE CAMERA IN A SLIGHTLY ROLLING FASHION. YOU CAN DUB ON A SHIP'S KLAXON SOUND. HEY, IF IT'S REALLY MEANT TO BE ROUGH OUT THERE YOU CAN HAVE HELPERS OFF CAMERA CHUCKING BUCKETS OF WATER AT THE CREW! (DON'T TELL THEM BEADLE SUGGESTED IT.)

WE CAN'T POSSIBLY COVER HERE ALL THE EXOTIC SETS AND LOCATIONS YOU MIGHT WANT TO CREATE, BUT THE PRINCIPLES ARE ALWAYS THE SAME. IT'S WORTH TAKING THE TIME TO IMAGINE THE LOCATION YOU WANT WITH ALL YOUR SENSES. NOTE DOWN THE SIGHTS AND SOUNDS YOU 'SEE' – AND USE THEM. THINK OF THE CLICHÉS ASSOCIATED WITH IT – AND USE THEM TO YOUR ADVANTAGE!

Holiday Videos

It used to be holiday snaps people dreaded. Now it's holiday videos. 'You must come round and see our holiday video' is an invitation guaranteed to strike fear into the hearts of even the closest of friends.

They know they're in for an hour and a half of unedited, un-thought-out aimless and wobbly shots of just about everything and anything you thought to film – not to mention unpalatable scenes (that seem to go on forever) of you in the skimpiest of briefs, which make them wish they hadn't eaten anything for the last week.

In a nutshell, most holiday videos are an endurance test.

But they don't have to be. The secret is to make something of them.

The Golden Rules of Holiday Videos

★Edit them down – and I mean right down – when you get home. Keep the full length versions to yourself – and don't inflict them on others. Use only your very best shots.

★Give them a structure – a beginning, middle and end.

★Add things to spice them up – like a voiceover commentary and music.

★Above all, make them funny and entertaining.

What Should You Shoot?

★ Don't forget – packing and preparations are all part of the holiday, so consider filming these as well.

★ The journey to your airport and the wait in the terminal is also part of the holiday. Be sensible. Don't shoot a spoof scene that involves running around Heathrow Terminal 4 with a fake gun yelling 'Allah al Aqaba!' – and be very wary of filming in foreign airports which may be touchy about security.

★ Don't plan important scenes that take place on the plane. Most airlines won't allow you to film on board. This is supposed to be because camcorders can interfere with sensitive electrical systems in the plane. That's total nonsense of course – the real reason is that their insurance companies don't want you to have visual proof of cracks in the fuselage or evidence of abominable in-flight food that might later lead to criminal prosecution. Still, filming on most flights is a no-no.

★ Shoot plenty of local colour – things that look visually interesting and capture the true feeling of the place. If you're going somewhere exotic, it's a waste just to shoot the family on the beach. Get all that wonderful local colour – lots of shots of surly-looking locals, defecating donkeys, street markets swarming with flies, wretched-looking children, dilapidated taxis and grubby buildings. Be up and about to film the genuine reaction of your family when the Imam wakes them up by calling the faithful to prayers at five in the morning (you might need to bleep the sound track later).

★ For best results, you should also think about shooting some running jokes. Does hubby like his food? Then make a point of showing him stuffing his face in some taverna or café every ten seconds. Get him to try and commentate on the holiday with his mouth full. Do the kids whinge? Cut all their best moans and groans into a fast and telling montage!

★ Hold competitions and video them. How about 'The World Bellyflop Olympics', 'The Silliest Way to Enter a Swimming Pool' or 'The World Record Splash Attempt' around the pool, or 'The World's Daftest Sandcastle' on the beach?

★ Have fun with the waiter. Go on – you're on holiday. Talk to him in utter gibberish and video him trying to be pleasant and understanding while getting progressively more baffled. This works fine for Spain. If you're in Blackpool, pretend to be foreign to wind your waiter up. I know it's naughty and I know it's wrong – but you'll get some great footage!

★ Film your return home, complete with your family's immediate reactions. Very telling!

DON'T GET CARRIED AWAY!

WHATEVER YOU DO, DON'T GET SO CONSUMED BY MAKING YOUR VIDEO THAT YOU ALLOW IT TO TAKE OVER YOUR ENTIRE HOLIDAY! YOU'RE MEANT TO BE ENJOYING A WELL-DESERVED BREAK. TURNING YOUR FAMILY'S ONLY VACATION OF THE YEAR INTO ONE LONG, INTERMINABLE LOCATION SHOOT WILL NOT MAKE YOU VERY POPULAR – ESPECIALLY IF THE REST OF YOUR FAMILY DOESN'T SHARE YOUR ENTHUSIASM FOR MAKING BLOCKBUSTERS!

Beadle Tip

THE NEXT TIME SOMEONE SHOWS YOU THEIR HOLIDAY VIDEO, PAY CAREFUL ATTENTION TO WHAT THEY'RE TALKING ABOUT. CHANCES ARE THEY'LL BE TELLING YOU ABOUT THE HILARIOUS WAITER THEY MET OR THAT BRILLIANT NIGHT AT THE DISCO – BUT THEY'RE SHOWING YOU PICTURES OF A SUNSET AND SOME PINK PUFFY BODIES IN FLIP-FLOPS STANDING ON THE BEACH. THEY HAVEN'T FILMED THE REALLY MEMORABLE THINGS! DON'T MAKE THE SAME MISTAKE.

Safety First

★It's very tempting to show off for the camera, especially on holiday. If you've never attempted a triple back flip off the high diving board before, don't do it now – or they'll be using the video at the inquest.

★Don't shoot any spoof comedy thrillers with titles like 'Break-in at a Turkish Air Force Base' or instructional films entitled 'How To Taunt the Local Police Militia'. Many countries have a funny attitude to law and order and filming around high security installations, and may decide to confiscate your camcorder or throw you in jail with three swarthy men of indeterminate sexual preferences. Or both.

★Some locals may not take too kindly to you filming them. You may think they look hilarious in that get-up. They don't. Some may even believe a camcorder can steal their souls – Parisians are funny that way. Be polite and use your common sense. Some colourfully dressed individuals may expect a few coins for the privilege of filming them. Pay them. They bite.

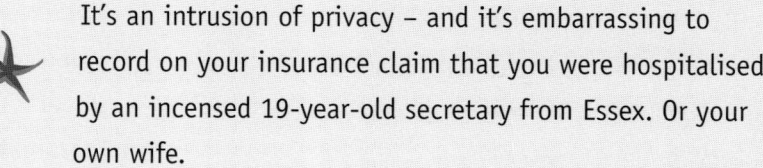

★Don't film topless women sunbathing on the beach. It's an intrusion of privacy – and it's embarrassing to record on your insurance claim that you were hospitalised by an incensed 19-year-old secretary from Essex. Or your own wife.

★Be careful about using your camcorder in any countries where there are more posters of the president on the streets than for Levi jeans. In these countries, never film a building with a tank parked outside it, no matter how historic it looks.

★If you can, be extra, extra careful when shooting on a beach. Camcorders hate heat. They also hate salt water and humidity – and there's probably plenty of both. Even a few particles of sand can cause damage. Always cover your camcorder up in between shots, preferably in a waterproof case.

Travelling Further

So far, we've really just talked about improving your family holiday video, but there's no reason why you can't write a Blockbuster which takes advantage of the unusual location you're visiting – and filming it while you're there. It'll make a change from filming it in the park or down the High Street!

The simplest kind of Blockbuster to make from your holiday is the spoof documentary:

Turn your holiday video into a spoof documentary

You can do this when you get home, reviewing all your shots and then writing a spoof voiceover to go over the best. There are lots of different approaches you can take with the same raw material. Some ideas you might like to consider include:

★A spoof travelogue – 'Blackpool – Land of Mystery'.

★An anthropological study of 'Brits Abroad'.

★A documentary narrated through the voice of a Greek islander sick to death of these tourists he's watching (practise your Stavros impersonation!).

★A local tourist board promotional film for their holiday paradise, praising every last little thing in bizarre pidgin English.

★Your children's thoughts on the holiday destination and the behaviour of their parents (be prepared to have your feelings hurt!).

ISLE OF WIGHT
The Land that
Time Forgot

Beadle Tips

★I KNOW IT SOUNDS OBVIOUS, BUT CHECK THAT YOUR CAMCORDER IS WORKING BEFORE YOU LEAVE. YOU DON'T WANT TO SPEND HALF YOUR HOLIDAY TRYING TO FIND THE ONLY CAMCORDER REPAIR FACILITY ON CRETE – AND THEN DISCOVERING IT'S CLOSED FOR THE SUMMER.

★BUY TAPES FOR YOUR CAMCORDER BEFORE YOU GO. BUYING THEM ABROAD CAN BE EXPENSIVE AND THEY MAY BE DIFFICULT TO FIND.

★IF YOU'RE GOING ON LOTS OF COACH TOURS OR YOU'VE GOT A HIRE CAR, SHOOT SOME SHOTS OF THE VEHICLE MOVING. YOU CAN USE THESE TO 'ESTABLISH' THE FACT THAT YOU'RE NOW OFF TO A NEW LOCATION.

Other types of blockbuster

Admit it – wouldn't that *Indiana Jones* spoof you've always wanted to do look great with the *real* pyramids in the background. Holidays give you the chance to make great-looking Blockbusters that you just can't achieve at home.

However, if you want to achieve this, the golden rule is 'think simple – and think short'. For starters, your cast and crew will probably be limited to the people you're travelling with, and you'll have much less technical support. You're not going to travel with lights, are you?

Beadle Tip

MOST COUNTRIES, QUITE INCONSIDERATELY, DON'T USE THE SAME 'NORMAL' MAINS POWER SUPPLY AS WE DO. THEY USE A STRANGE FOREIGN ONE INSTEAD. UNLESS YOU'VE GOT BAGS AND BAGS OF SPARE, FULLY CHARGED CAMCORDER BATTERIES WITH YOU, YOU'LL NEED TO BUY AN ADAPTER FOR YOUR RECHARGER AND POSSIBLY A TRANSFORMER TOO.

You may not even want to lug a tripod about, let alone a suitcase full of props and costumes . . .

You're also not likely to be able to sort out permissions, so you'll have to shoot on the sly. A full set-up with tripod and reflector, plus two people in gorilla costumes wrestling with a third dressed as a ballet dancer is going to attract unwanted attention. Be discreet. Avoid filming a Blockbuster that draws attention to yourself. Look as if you're just a tourist filming the usual tourist things. That way you won't have to bung the local gendarmes half of your Thomas Cook traveller's cheques to leave you alone.

That said, what sort of Blockbuster should you be thinking of? Ideally, something which takes full advantage of your location. If you could film the Blockbuster just as well at home, why film it during your precious holiday? Consider a comedy sketch set around a hotel swimming pool or a Shirley-Valentine-type skit set in an enchanting harbourside café. Maybe it's a romantic tryst in the shadow of the Eiffel Tower.

Maybe you'll want to make an over-enthusiastic 'Five Go Adventuring' style spoof – 'Five Go to Marbella'.

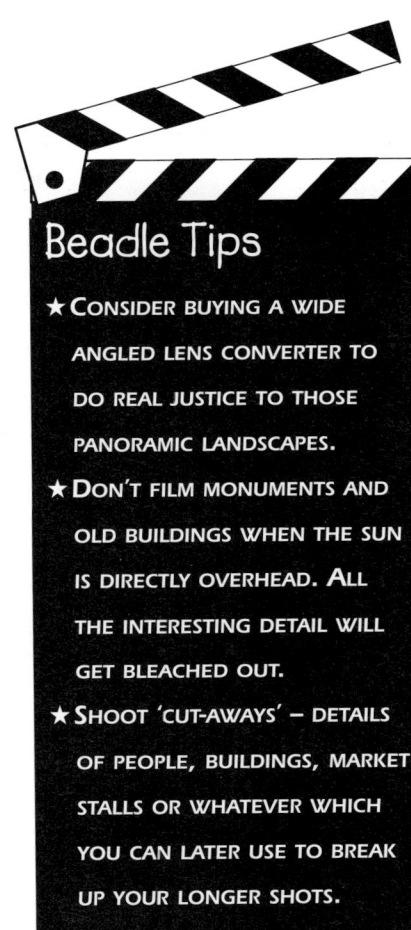

Building Your Own Stock Footage Library

Even if the last thing on your mind while on holiday is making a Blockbuster, consider filming interesting things that you come across – local colour, exotic sunsets, the ocean, famous landmarks etc., and add them to your own video library.

One day, you may want to use that footage as establishing scenes for a Blockbuster shot closer to home!

Wedding Videos

If friends are relying on you to video their wedding for them, they're probably expecting a straightforward wedding souvenir, trusting you to produce a quality record of the big day which they can treasure forever.

They will not thank you if they think you're making a straightforward wedding video, only to find you've turned it into a gothic horror movie. Worse, you've superimposed the caption 'Bride of Frankenstein' over the bride. There will be tears. There will be raised voices. There may even be physical acts of a painful nature. Remember, camcorders do not work well after being forced into a body cavity. In these circumstances, film the occasion sensibly. Produce that video they'll be proud to send to Cousin Jack in Australia.

Remember that a wedding isn't just the service. It's the preparations by bride and groom. It's the arrival at the church, synagogue or registry office or wherever. It's the happy crowd scenes and the posing for photographs after the service, the journey on to the reception afterwards and the reception itself. It's excited children, resplendent in their bridesmaid and page boy outfits. It's elderly relatives blowing their noses into hankies, and desperately wrinkly grannies looking baffled and submerged inside warm coats. Go for the colour as well as the events, and you'll capture something really special. Use that tripod for the set shots, but you'll capture the really telling moments best by 'shooting from the hip'. Hold the camera steady.

In the church, no one will thank you if you keep clumping around and wrestling with the tripod during the ceremony, so pick one set spot, preferably at the front and to the side where you can capture the couple and the vicar, and also reaction from the guests in the pews. There's nothing worse than a wedding video shot from the back of a church which is just thirty minutes' worth of the backs of people's heads.

Don't get so close as to be a nuisance, but make sure you're close enough to pick up the sound. Churches with their wide high ceilings are usually very echoey, so you'd be best using a microphone positioned somewhat closer to the couple than you are.

Be prepared to make a full day of it – and for goodness' sake carry a few spare fully charged batteries. They're not going to put everything on hold while you jump in a taxi and head for the nearest camcorder speciality shop!

If you like, having done the job 'properly' you can always re-edit and shoot extra scenes to produce a second, 'less conventional' piece to suit you.

If someone else is making the official wedding video, then you can afford to lark around and perhaps produce a quirky Blockbuster as a gift to the couple – an alternative 'unofficial' wedding video. Now you can concentrate on the drunken behaviour at the reception, the gorging of food by greedy relatives, the best man pestering the bridesmaids for sexual favours and the altercation with the caterers behind the scenes. A voiceover works well with this type of film, either naïvely gushing in style or cynical and knowing. The choice is yours.

A wedding is also usually a spectacular occasion. You might want to use it just as a backdrop to your Blockbuster. Suppose you were making a comedy thriller called 'My Caterer, My Killer' or 'Cake of Death' about a company of homicidal caterers who poison guests at every function they attend. You could film the action in the kitchens, or in an ante-room at an earlier or later date, and use cut-aways of the real wedding and reception as if the two were happening simultaneously – not something you could achieve otherwise without a huge cast and budget!

Beadle Tips

★ REMEMBER YOU WILL NEED TO GET PERMISSION TO SHOOT A CHURCH WEDDING. MANY VICARS DO NOT LIKE THE IDEA OF FILMING INSIDE THEIR CHURCH, OR MAY ONLY ALLOW IT UNDER STRICTLY CONTROLLED CIRCUMSTANCES.

★ PLAN AHEAD AND WORK OUT WHERE YOU NEED TO BE – AND WHEN. YOU ONLY GET ONE CRACK AT FILMING THIS!

★ SOME CHURCHES HAVE THEIR OWN IN-BUILT AUDIO SYSTEMS. YOU MAY BE ABLE TO TAKE AN AUDIO 'FEED' IN FROM THIS TO YOUR CAMCORDER TO HELP YOU GET BETTER SOUND.

★ IF YOU CAN, WANGLE YOURSELF AN INVITE TO THE REHEARSAL FOR THE WEDDING CEREMONY. YOU CAN USE IT TO FIND THE RIGHT POSITION AND SUSS OUT THE SOUND AND LIGHTING. FILM IT TOO. IT'LL MAKE A NICE LITTLE 'BEHIND THE SCENES' OPENING SEQUENCE FOR THE 'REAL' WEDDING CEREMONY.

Cruel but Funny

At a church wedding, many guests don't know the words of the hymns. But they don't like to just stand there, so they mime. Badly. Very badly indeed. While filming, pan the camera around, pick out the mimers and zoom right in on them. It's cruel – but it's hilarious viewing!

Unusual Positions

If you're not the official wedding video maker, you can afford to film a decidedly different take on events. Get into unusual positions. For example, go to the car park before the wedding and film the guests arriving. They've often travelled a long way, so they'll walk around funny trying to stretch their stiff legs, or adjust their bunched-up fine clothing in all kinds of undignified ways!

Always talk to the best man beforehand, and try to find out what pranks he and his mates are planning. That way you can have the camcorder set up perfectly to record the whole thing. If he's going to be pulling out props during his speech, find out what, where and when, so you can have your shot wide enough to cover the action, instead of missing it because you're tight in on his face.

Conventional wedding shots are all very well...but go for the behind the scenes shots too...

Unique Wedding Gifts

★People have had camcorders for well over a decade. There's an awful lot of video footage available of people growing up – and before camcorders, of course, every family used to have a Super 8 cine camera to record the children.

Why not get in contact with the bride and groom's parents and see what they've got available? You could put it together and create a wonderful account of their lives to date, culminating, of course, in their marriage. You can either video Super 8 film as it's projected on a screen or have it professionally transferred. You can also film still photographs (to add 'life' to them, try slowly panning across the image with a tripod or zooming in or out).

I needn't add that you can either make your film touching and sentimental or jokey and satirical. For the finishing touch, you can add a spoken commentary or music – or both.

★At the reception, set your camcorder up in a quiet location well away from the drunken revelry. Invite each guest to come up to be taped, either one at a time, or as couples and families, throughout the event. Ask each to wish the happy couple well – or to recall a funny story about them. Ask them leading questions like 'What's the one thing you'll never forget about the groom?' or 'Is she too good for him?' With a little editing afterwards, you can present the happy couple with a personal and totally unique video wedding card!

Extra naughty option: Re-dub your questions later so the answer to how long were they engaged for ('5 months') becomes the answer to your new question, 'How pregnant is she?' . . .

★Why not film a surprise *This is Your Life* episode about the happy couple, complete with host and big red book? You can use old video or cine footage of them, and intersperse this with filmed messages or reminiscences from parents, relatives, friends and workmates.

Beadle Tips

★ SO THE VICAR SAID NO. DON'T DESPAIR. YOU CAN STILL DO A SNEAKY SOUND RECORDING OF EVENTS AND THEN DUB THEM OVER EXTERIOR SCENES OF THE CHURCH OR CLOSE-UPS OF THE HAPPY COUPLE TO GIVE A FEELING FOR THE CEREMONY.

★ DON'T GET IN THE WAY OF THE OFFICIAL WEDDING VIDEO MAKER OR THE PHOTOGRAPHER. WEDDINGS CAN BE SPOILED BY AN UNSIGHTLY PUNCH-UP.

★ FILL YOUR POCKETS WITH SPARE TAPES AND BATTERIES. YOU'LL SHOOT MUCH MORE THAN YOU THINK YOU WILL.

★ GET DOWN AND FUNKY ON THE DANCE FLOOR DURING THE RECEPTION. USE ALL THOSE WACKY SHOTS YOU'VE SEEN ON TOP OF THE POPS AND CONSIDER SPECIAL ATTACHMENTS LIKE STARBURST FILTERS AS WELL. YOU'LL TURN GRANDAD INTO A STAR!

Children's Birthday Parties

Children's birthday parties are magic little moments, full of funny incidents, sudden tears and angelic faces smeared with chocolate. They are, as any parent will tell you, almost impossible to control.

Chances are, you'll want a straightforward account of little Sarah's fifth birthday party. That's your reason for filming it, pure and simple. You're not going to try to turn it into a spoof of *Village of the Damned* or *Lord of the Flies*. If you are, you'll wreck the occasion, you won't get the results you're looking for and your daughter won't speak to you for weeks afterwards. So, how do you go about making a better children's birthday party video?

Editing Your Party Video

★Structure your video with a beginning, middle and end.

★Keep it reasonably short. Use all the best bits, the special moments. A single wide shot of undisciplined children running about madly for no discernible reason can get wearing on the viewer after ten minutes!

★One of the biggest problems you'll find is with the sound, especially if there's music playing in the background. It may jump abruptly as you cut backwards and forwards in time. You can dub music over the sequence later or use general excited kids' sounds with no music from elsewhere on your tape.

★Alternatively, use a well-known children's song as the soundtrack (something from an animated feature is ideal). Timing your video to a particular song is a good discipline to make sure your party video isn't over long.

★Keep using cut-aways to faces. Children's faces are just about the most photogenic things in the world, and they'll help break up the shots of general chaos.

★Get your birthday boy or girl to draw and write their open captions to title the video. Alternatively if the cake says 'Happy 5th Birthday, Sarah' on it – then why not use a shot of that as your opening title?

Beadle Tip

ALL TOO OFTEN, WE FILM SMALL CHILDREN FROM AN ADULT'S PERSPECTIVE. WE LOOK DOWN ON THEM. THIS ISN'T THE BEST ANGLE TO CAPTURE WHAT MAKES CHILDREN SO SPECIAL. TRY SETTING YOUR CAMERA TRIPOD LOW, SO THAT THE CAMERA IS AT THEIR EYE LEVEL. IT'LL REALLY BRING THE PARTY TO LIFE!

Children's Birthday Parties – A Shot Check List

★Capture all the hard work the parents put in. Film the making of the cake and the trifles, the wrapping of the presents and the 'pass the parcel'.

★Shoot the food table perfectly laid out.

★Film your child waiting for her friends to arrive. Capture the eagerness and the excitement.

★Shoot children arriving with their parents to be dropped off. Capture the kids struggling out of their coats and passing their presents over.

★Now capture as much as you can of the mayhem which ensues. Take the time and trouble to get lots of close-ups of kids' faces – the guests' as well as your own child's. You can use them as cut-aways when you're editing and they look great, as well as providing a refreshing contrast to the wider shot of two dozen tots running about and yelling in all directions.

★If there's a children's entertainer try and capture shots of him/her performing and the looks of wonder and amazement on the children's faces as they watch even the simplest and most obvious conjuring tricks.

★Find children who look mischievous. They probably are – and they'll probably do or say something you'll be thrilled to get on video.

★The funniest material you'll probably get is from the kids themselves. Interview them. Ask them questions about themselves and the party – what they want to be when they grow up, etc. (Be gentle. Asking them questions like: 'Do you really like the birthday girl or are you just here for the jelly?' and 'Who do you think smells at this party?' can create a full scale riot in double quick time.)

★Film the eating. It's quite amazing. Go for close-ups on those

Beadle Tip

DON'T TRY TO VIDEO THE PARTY AND CONTROL IT AT THE SAME TIME. MAKE SURE THERE'S ANOTHER RESPONSIBLE ADULT AROUND TO TAKE CHARGE WHILE YOU'RE FILMING!

spoons being shovelled at a rate of knots into busy little mouths. Find the muckiest child and film him as he disappears under layers of caked-on food.

★ Don't forget the blowing out of the candles and the traditional singing of 'Happy Birthday to You'.

★ Film the remnants of the table afterwards from exactly the same position and with exactly the same frame as you did the table earlier in the day. Join the before and after shots later on in the edit to show just what the little monsters have done.

★ Film the parents collecting their children.

★ Shoot the mess in your living room, the cleaning up afterwards and the exhausted parents flopping down after dealing with the devastation.

★ End up on a nice long close-up shot of your child, asleep.

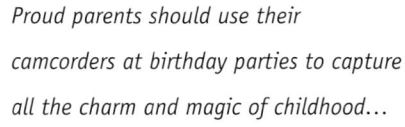

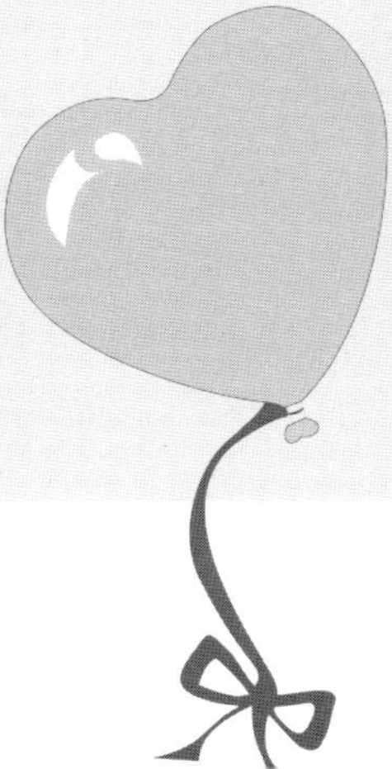

Proud parents should use their camcorders at birthday parties to capture all the charm and magic of childhood...

Blowing Out the Candles – A Piece of Cake!

When you're filming your child blowing out the candles on the birthday cake, don't go too close in. Camcorders hate fire and the flames can 'burn' a nasty after image into the tape.

Also, be aware that, if your child's sitting down to blow out the candles and you're standing up, all you're likely to get is a shot of the top of their head! Come down to 'cake level' as we say in the business and shoot through and up.

Video Birthday Cards

Why not create a superb and very individual souvenir of their birthday for your child? Set your camcorder up on a tripod in a quiet corner. Then, as each partygoer turns up, sit them down in the same place and get them to wish your son or daughter a very happy birthday. Cut them all together at the end and your child will have a wonderful video birthday card to treasure, featuring all of their friends!

Christmas Camcorder Capers

All too often, camcorder owners think videoing Christmas is just about capturing the kids opening their presents. That's a shame, because you can do much more:

★Video all the preparations on Christmas Eve – writing the notes to Santa, leaving out the milk and biscuits for him and so on. Ask your children for their opinions on Santa, Rudolph and the gang.

★Hide your camcorder in the children's bedroom. Kiss them goodnight, 'accidentally' leave the light on and film them talking eagerly about Santa's visit and the toys they're hoping for. You can return ten minutes later to turn the light off and sneakily retrieve the camera.

★When Santa visits your house to deliver the presents and take the children's milk and biscuits, why not video him in the act! The kids will be thrilled to see Santa in their own home when you show it to them on Christmas Day.

★In the Beadle household, we have a tradition of hiding little presents around the house and our children spend part of Christmas morning tracking them down! This kind of treasure hunt is great fun for them – and great fun to video as well!

Ho, ho, video!

Proper Props

If you've been brought up on a diet of *Blue Peter* and *Vision On* then improvising props shouldn't pose too many problems. Equally, if you're reasonably adept at DIY then you'll positively relish the chance to make realistic papier mâché boulders or a balsa wood skyscraper.

Waste Not, Want Not

To the inspired amateur video maker, the tube from a fluorescent light and a toilet roll are the basis for a *Star Wars* light sabre; an old broom stick, a pair of headphones and a large paper plate will make a mine detector, while a Coke can painted green with a plastic film canister stuck on the top is a deadly radioactive isotope.

To make props, collect scrap of all kinds. I don't mean you should buy a horse and cart and go collecting old iron bedsteads or radiators door-to-

A sliced-up rubbish bin, a few sticky stars and some old tin foil and it's 'goodbye, uninteresting mutt' and 'hello, Space Dog Calypso – Empress of the Canine Star Amazons'

door. No, the sort of things you'll find useful are the items most households throw away each week as a matter of course.

Other sources of useful materials are shops and supermarkets. They have large waste bins round the back and these can be a gold mine for large pieces of corrugated card, hardboard, string, boxes and polystyrene of various shapes and sorts.

Do ask permission first, though, or else they'll call the police – or take pity on you and bring you out a large box of date-expired Mr Kipling Bakewell tarts to take back with you and share with everyone in cardboard city.

The Prop Maker's Two Best Friends

I'm not talking about your mates Jeff and Liz who own Props-R-Us (useful though they are) – but papier mâché and wire mesh (chicken wire).

Separately, both these materials are useful for making props but together they're unbeatable. Use the chicken wire to make a rough framework of whatever shape you're trying to construct – it could be a false arm, a statue, a huge potty, a stone column, a torpedo, fake branches etc., then use the papier mâché to cover it, and give you a firm surface ready for painting. (For larger objects you might need a wooden base to keep them stable.)

How to make papier mâché

Tear newspaper into small pieces from 2" x 1" to 4" x 3", depending on the area you need to cover. Soak them in cold water paste (wallpaper paste is ideal) and lay them over the chicken wire until it's completely covered. When one layer is dry, cover them with a second – and so on until you've built up four or five layers of paper.

How to make chicken wire

You don't. You buy it (from pet shops, hardware shops, garden centres and DIY stores).

Beadle Tips

★ IF YOU WANT TO MAKE THINGS LOOK LIKE METAL: USE TIN FOIL, METALLIC SPRAY PAINT, MILK BOTTLE TOPS, METALLIC CARD.

★ IF YOU WANT TO MAKE THINGS LOOK LIKE WOOD: DIP A BRUSH IN A RATHER DRY BROWN WATER PAINT, OR A THICK MIXTURE OF COFFEE/HOT CHOCOLATE POWDER AND WATER. USE THE BRUSH LIGHTLY AND THE PAINT SPARINGLY.

TRY COLLECTING . . .

PLASTIC BOTTLES AND CONTAINERS	MILK CARTONS	BOTTLE TOPS
BISCUIT TINS	NEWSPAPERS	CARDBOARD TUBES
WRAPPING PAPER	EGG BOXES	PLASTIC CUTLERY
COAT HANGERS	PAPER BAGS	TOOTHPASTE DISPENSERS
STRING	CARDBOARD BOXES	TIN FOIL
OLD LIGHT BULBS	BITS OF WIRE	TIN CANS

FAST FOOD POLYSTYRENE CARTONS AND CUPS

Turning the Familiar into the Unfamiliar

Apart from constructing props from waste materials you should also try and look at everyday objects in a new light. It's amazing how, with a few alterations and a lick of paint, these can be utilised in a completely new way. Using your imagination like this is a good exercise in lateral thinking. Here's an example:

21 uses of a plastic football

1. A bomb (paint it black and stick on a cotton reel with a piece of string on the top as a fuse)

2. Join loads of them together with short pieces of wooden dowelling to make a huge model of the DNA helix

3. Paint it red to make an immense mutated Dutch cheese (it'll probably taste as good)

4. Get five of them, some string and a wooden framework to make an over-sized executive toy (a useful prop in your interpretation of Jack and the Beanstalk where the giant is a Finance Director of a large corporation)

5. Paint it bright red and put it on top of a wooden pole to make a large lollipop

6. Paint it silver to make a large ball bearing

7. Paint it brown to make a giant Malteser (for 'Attack Of The Mutant Maltesers' possibly)

8. Thread several together on a thick piece of string to make a large set of beads (for 'Attack Of The Mutant Rosaries' possibly)

9. Paint it yellow, hang it from the ceiling and use as a model of the s⟨...⟩ (or moon)

10. Paint it a different colour and use it as a model of another planet (for Saturn, use a large card disc or an old LP with a large hole cut in the middle)

11. Cover it with torn newspaper and paint it green to resemble a giant Brussels sprout

12. Paint it suppository colour and use as a comedy suppository

13. Stuff it up the front of someone's clothing to make them look pregnant (or fat)

14. Stuff it up the back of someone's clothing to make them look like Quasimodo

15. Paint it red and attach it to the back of your neck to represent a nasty boil

16. Paint two of them black, fix them on to a short piece of broomstick and use as barbells

17. Paint it to look like a huge eyeball

18. Stick two short, thin beanpoles through the centre so it looks like a satellite

19. Get two of them and cut out holes for your feet; wear as shoes of the future

20. Cut it in half, turn it inside out to make a bald wig

21. A football

WARNING!!

IN MAKING PROPS YOU'LL BE USING GLUES, KNIVES, SCISSORS, SAWS AND ALL SORTS OF OTHER SHARP OR SPIKY ITEMS. USE THEM RESPONSIBLY AND CAREFULLY AND, IF NECESSARY, GET ADULT SUPERVISION.

Costumes

If I had to choose between making props or costumes completely from scratch I'd choose props any day, for these reasons:

✂ It's much harder to make convincing entire costumes from raw materials than it is props.

✂ Costumes tend to be in shot longer, and more prominently, so that any defects are much more likely to be seen.

✂ Because they're subject to much more wear and tear than props, there's a high risk of bits falling off home-made costumes.

✂ I can't sew.

Of course, the need for costumes all depends on the script you've written. If you want to avoid the cost of hiring costumes or the trouble of making them, don't give yourself problems by deciding to make the following Blockbusters:

★ 'Godzilla versus Jabba the Hut'

★ 'The Black Knight Meets the Frankenstein Sextuplets'

★ 'Teletubby Chainsaw Massacre' (much as I'd pay good money to see it)

On the other hand, I'm not saying that your video should just involve the invisible man talking to himself. No, when it comes to costumes, the answer is to start with the basics and *accessorise*.

What do I mean by that? Well, for instance, add material or bits and pieces to clothes – usually jackets – to make them look less

Not a looney but a fearless astronaut, courtesy of a coat with a shiny lining turned inside-out, washing-up gloves and a bucket covered in tin foil

100

ordinary. For example, you can turn one of your dad's old dinner suits into an admiral's jacket by first putting some thick yellow wool or gold embossed foil (the type that goes round the sides of birthday cakes) round the cuffs to look like military braid. Complete the effect by covering the buttons with gold milk bottle tops and making medal ribbon out of card which you stick on to the breast pocket.

You'd be surprised how flexible some items of clothing are. Charity shops are a wonderful source for clothes of all descriptions. Cut them up, dye them, decorate them, sew items together, take them in, let them out, shorten, lengthen – use your imagination! Even something as simple as turning a jacket inside out to reveal a shiny and possibly brightly coloured lining can make the wearer look like a TV game show host.

Two Very Adaptable Items of Clothing

Here are two perennially useful items of clothing which no amateur video maker should be without:

One-piece dark coloured overalls

These are one of the most versatile items of clothing. Apart from being able to play car mechanics and decorators, with the addition of a few badges you could take on the role of a whole host of much more exotic occupations: SWAT team member, toxic waste handler, pilot, astronaut, tank commander, bomb disposal expert, saboteur, even the man who services the lasers on X-Wing Fighters.

White warehouse coats

Although not as adaptable as the above, these are still pretty useful for scientists (both the sane and mad varieties), doctors, mortuary workers, lab assistants, butchers and technicians.

In addition, worn back to front with your arms tied behind your back, they make a great straitjacket.

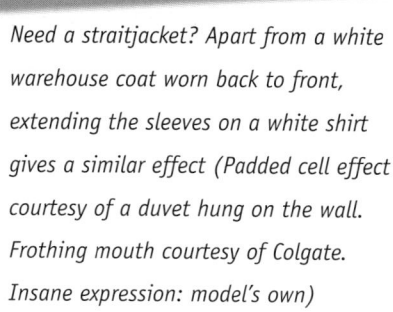

Need a straitjacket? Apart from a white warehouse coat worn back to front, extending the sleeves on a white shirt gives a similar effect (Padded cell effect courtesy of a duvet hung on the wall. Frothing mouth courtesy of Colgate. Insane expression: model's own)

101

Rehearsals

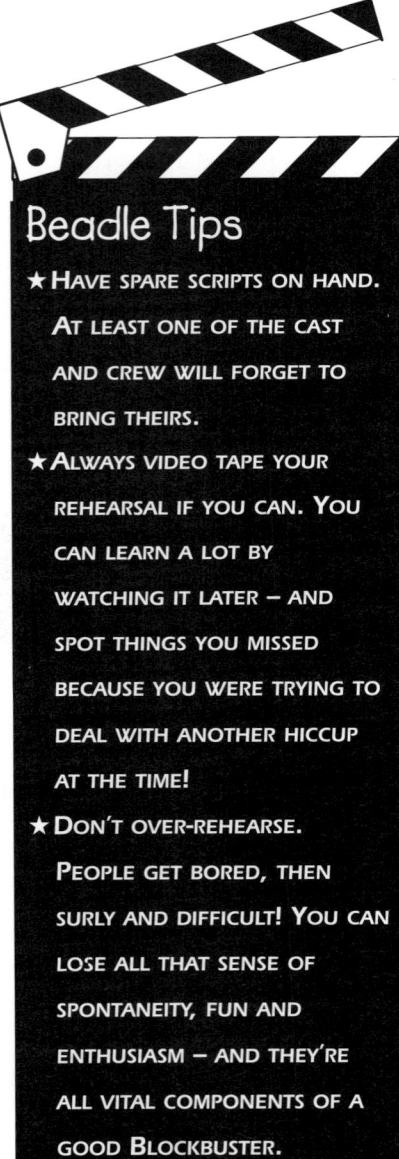

Admit it. You're tempted to skip this section of the book. You want to get out there and start taping right away. Don't. (And anyway, it's only a short section.)

You'll learn a lot from holding a rehearsal. You'll find out which lines are difficult for the actors to say, which props are problematic, which costume is going to split right down the back as soon as the actor bends over, which camera shots don't work and who's likely to let you down by not turning up on the day.

Where to Hold Your Rehearsals

In an ideal world, you'd rehearse using the sets and locations you'll be using on the day. In practice, this might be impossible. It doesn't matter. Hold the rehearsal in your living room or your back garden for now. What's important is that everyone understands what it is they have to do on the day.

When to Hold Your Rehearsals

This may come as a surprise, but your Blockbuster isn't the most important thing in the world to your cast and crew. They've got lives (well, except for your sad brother-in-law). Rehearse them too early and they'll forget everything. Absolutely everything.

On the other hand, hold a rehearsal on the eve of shooting and you may not have time to put problems with script, costumes, props etc. right before the big day.

If you can, rehearse on the weekend before you intend to start. That way, you have all the time you need for the rehearsal *and* for putting things right.

Beadle Tips

★ HAVE SPARE SCRIPTS ON HAND. AT LEAST ONE OF THE CAST AND CREW WILL FORGET TO BRING THEIRS.

★ ALWAYS VIDEO TAPE YOUR REHEARSAL IF YOU CAN. YOU CAN LEARN A LOT BY WATCHING IT LATER — AND SPOT THINGS YOU MISSED BECAUSE YOU WERE TRYING TO DEAL WITH ANOTHER HICCUP AT THE TIME!

★ DON'T OVER-REHEARSE. PEOPLE GET BORED, THEN SURLY AND DIFFICULT! YOU CAN LOSE ALL THAT SENSE OF SPONTANEITY, FUN AND ENTHUSIASM — AND THEY'RE ALL VITAL COMPONENTS OF A GOOD BLOCKBUSTER.

What to Do at Your Rehearsal

★Make sure you've got all the props for the actors and get them into costume if possible. Remember that people in costume or wearing masks often feel 'hidden' and are more willing to let themselves go. If Cousin Bob gets used to wearing that ballerina costume now, he won't feel quite so self-conscious when you're filming in the shopping precinct.

★It's very useful if your cast have learned their lines by this stage, so that they can concentrate on their movements and handling their props, but it's not essential.

★Make rehearsals fun – but keep control of them or they'll turn into a party. Have some drinks and some snacks laid on and work out an itinerary of everything you want to achieve in advance:

★Start with a read-through with your cast. Take notes on where they stumble. Listen to your lines. Can you improve them? Does Grandad really have to say: 'Round and round the rugged rock the ragged rascal ran?' – with his false teeth?

★Next, practise each scene one by one – getting the cast to do the moves you want as they say their lines. Use all the props. The technical crew should be watching this to understand what they need to be capturing. Make any changes you want to make as you go.

★Hold a brief discussion. Ask for suggestions. Find out if anyone has any worries. Then praise everyone to the Heavens. They're doing you a favour. So be nice. Don't lose your patience, even if the rehearsal has been less than successful – and don't say anything like:

– *'No! No! No! I told you, do it like this! Are you stupid or something?*

– *'God I hate working with amateurs!'*

– *'Well . . . that stank!'*

– *'Mess up once more, Granny – and you're out!'*

– *'You'll never work in this town again!'*

or you could find yourself looking for some new cast and crew!

Re-writing the Script

You know it was perfect the first time. I know it was perfect the first time. But, somehow or other, bits of it just seem wrong now. Those lines you'd imagined in the mouth of Julia Roberts sound wrong for some reason coming from Auntie Joan.

Don't be afraid to re-write. If an actor has a problem with delivering a line at rehearsals, chances are they'll make a hash of it on the day too. So find a line they *can* say.

Everyone who has ever worked in pantomime knows that the longer a show runs, the funnier it gets. This is because the cast keeps adding fresh new ad-libs. Don't be afraid to accept suggestions from your cast and crew on how to improve the script. Incorporate their ad-libs – and ask for their ideas. They may think of another joke you can add or – curses – a better joke than the one you've got!

Planning Your Shooting Schedule

You've had your big idea, written your script, decided on your locations and drawn up your storyboard. Now you have to decide which order to shoot your shots in.

You have a choice. You can either tape all your shots in the order they appear in the script and save yourself the task of editing your Blockbuster together later – or you can shoot your shots in the most convenient order and assemble them later.

If you're a little nervous about the process of editing, shooting everything in order can seem very appealing. In reality though, it can be very fiddly, very limiting and very, very time consuming.

Let's have a closer look at 'in-camera editing' now, as this process is usually called.

In-Camera Editing

This is the most simple form of editing you can choose. In fact, you're not even editing at all. You shoot all your shots in order as you go so that, at the end of production, everything is already assembled and complete inside your camcorder and ready to show.

Did I say simple? Well, it is in theory . . .

Imagine you're taking your fourth shot of the production. An actor makes a mistake. A dog barks off camera. An actor barks off camera. For whatever reason, the shot is ruined. You now rewind to the end of the last shot and shoot the scene again – but how accurate were you when you rewound the tape? Oh dear. Not very. You've rubbed out half of Steve's speech. The very speech he took fourteen takes to get right. So you have to go back and shoot *that* shot all over again.

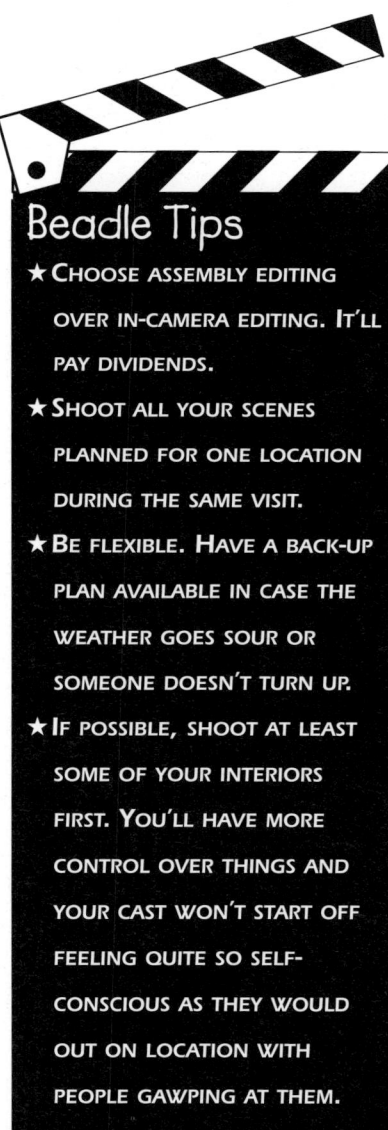

Beadle Tips

★ CHOOSE ASSEMBLY EDITING OVER IN-CAMERA EDITING. IT'LL PAY DIVIDENDS.

★ SHOOT ALL YOUR SCENES PLANNED FOR ONE LOCATION DURING THE SAME VISIT.

★ BE FLEXIBLE. HAVE A BACK-UP PLAN AVAILABLE IN CASE THE WEATHER GOES SOUR OR SOMEONE DOESN'T TURN UP.

★ IF POSSIBLE, SHOOT AT LEAST SOME OF YOUR INTERIORS FIRST. YOU'LL HAVE MORE CONTROL OVER THINGS AND YOUR CAST WON'T START OFF FEELING QUITE SO SELF-CONSCIOUS AS THEY WOULD OUT ON LOCATION WITH PEOPLE GAWPING AT THEM.

Basically, in-camera editing is OK if you're planning a very simple production with a single location, but otherwise you really should use another method.

ALLOWING FOR TIME

PROFESSIONALS ARE USUALLY PLEASED IF THEY GET **2–3** MINUTES 'IN THE CAN' PER DAY IN ONE LOCATION. YOU CAN PROBABLY BE MORE AMBITIOUS, BUT STILL ERR ON THE SIDE OF CAUTION. DON'T BE OVER-AMBITIOUS. CHANCES ARE, EVEN IF YOU'RE A 'ONE TAKE WONDER', GRANDAD WON'T BE. HE'LL BE A 'NINE TAKE NUISANCE'. SETTING THINGS UP ALWAYS TAKES LONGER THAN YOU THINK IT WILL AND THEN THERE'S TIME SPENT TRAVELLING BETWEEN LOCATIONS, SHOTS THAT GO WRONG, COFFEE BREAKS, PEOPLE TURNING UP LATE AND ALL KINDS OF THINGS THAT CAN EAT INTO YOUR SCHEDULE.

Why You Shouldn't Rely on In-Camera Editing

Alfred Hitchcock never did it. Oliver Stone doesn't do it. Steven Spielberg wouldn't dream of it. James Cameron just laughs. This is because they are really Time Lords.

And you're a Time Lord too. I don't mean that you live in a cheap set, fight cardboard monsters and the BBC hates you. I have no idea if any of these things apply to you. What I mean is that, as a director, you can manipulate Time and Space.

All movies are illusions. Here's an example. A car chase. We see a shot of a police car coming tearing around the corner and then cut to the next shot of the two police officers inside the car talking into a radio. Those two shots that appear to be happening sequentially could in fact have been taken days, weeks, even months apart.

But the audience can't tell that. They see the two shots juxtaposed and their brains make the assumption the director wants. You can outsmart your audience just as easily.

Assembly editing – that is, putting together all the shots of your Blockbuster later on – offers you all kinds of advantages that you might not think of at first.

Advantage 1: save time

Think about the following:

★ Shot 1 – Factory gates
★ Shot 2 – Girl waiting outside a cinema
★ Shot 3 – Factory gates again
★ Shot 4 – Girl outside cinema, looking at her watch.

Think what it would take to shoot just that very simple sequence in order if you were planning an in-camera edit. Do you really want to drive between the factory and the cinema twice? Think of the petrol. Think of the traffic. Think of how you'll feel when you discover that a whacking great juggernaut has parked across the factory gates while you were away!

Wouldn't it be more sensible to shoot all the shots at the factory location at the same time, and all the cinema shots together?

With assembly editing you can take all your shots in one location on a single visit.

Advantage 2: flexibility if circumstances change

Suppose you're planning on shooting on location – and it's hammering down with rain. If you're editing in-camera, you have to wait for the rain to stop. Maybe it will. Maybe it won't. If you're planning to edit later, you can switch plans and film your interior shots in the warm and dry now.

Beadle Tip

WHEN YOU'VE WORKED OUT YOUR SHOOTING SCHEDULE, GIVE ALL YOUR CAST AND CREW A COPY SO THAT THEY KNOW WHEN AND WHERE THEY'RE MEANT TO BE. THEN THERE'S NO EXCUSE . . .

Advantage 3: fitting in with awkward friends

Your mate Steve is in shot one, doing his best impression of John Travolta strutting down the street. Unfortunately, he can't make your first day of shooting this Saturday as it's an away match. He won't be available until Sunday. If you're planning to edit in-camera, that's the whole of Saturday gone for a burton then. You won't be able to start until Sunday.

If, on the other hand, you're assembly editing, you can film the shots without Steve on the Saturday and then shoot your opening scene the next day.

Shot Logging

If you plan to shoot your video out of sequence it's essential to make a note of all the shots you film – as you film them. This is called a 'shot log' and it's used to find the shots you want when it comes to editing.

When you log the shots, include as much information about them as possible. It's no good just listing:

★Shot 13, Take 1: Cousin Adam slips over

★Shot 13, Take 2: Cousin Adam slips over again

★Shot 13, Take 3: Cousin Adam slips over for the third time

All this tells you is that you have three shots of Cousin Adam falling over (we hope intentionally) – and nothing to differentiate them.

No, to make editing easier and quickly, list the following details (obviously, it will be easier if you have someone on the shoot to do this for you).

Shot and take number

List these numerically.

Time counter reading at the beginning of shot

Some camcorders offer this facility. If yours does, use it.

Description of shot

Don't be tempted to write things like 'Brill!', 'Spielberg-esque' or 'Hollywood here I come!' Here you should write 'Close-up', 'Panoramic view', 'Slow pan left–right', 'Pull out to reveal banana skin' etc.

Special comments

This is where you can add useful comments such as 'Blue filter used', 'Loud aircraft noise' etc., but equally this is the section where you should be the most critical, for instance, listing things like 'Out of focus', 'Camera fell over' etc.

Remember your shot log is to help you find the best shots for your final edit – the more information you log now means the less time you have to spend searching through the tape(s) at the edit stage.

Continuity

When you change shots and locations it's easy to get confused about what your characters were wearing or doing. Did Auntie Adie wear the red scarf or the blue one? Did Uncle David mince along with his hand on his left hip or his right hip?

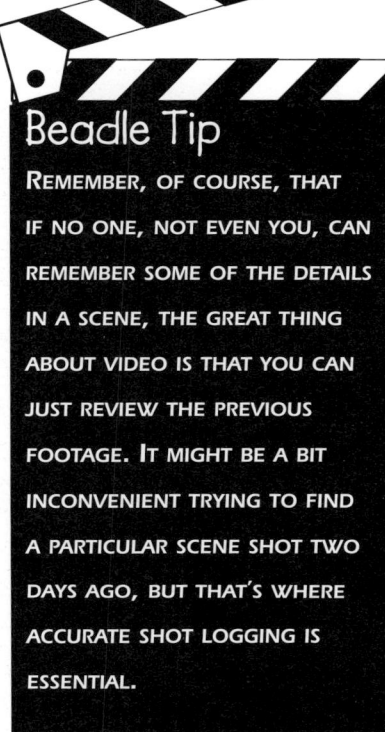

Beadle Tip

REMEMBER, OF COURSE, THAT IF NO ONE, NOT EVEN YOU, CAN REMEMBER SOME OF THE DETAILS IN A SCENE, THE GREAT THING ABOUT VIDEO IS THAT YOU CAN JUST REVIEW THE PREVIOUS FOOTAGE. IT MIGHT BE A BIT INCONVENIENT TRYING TO FIND A PARTICULAR SCENE SHOT TWO DAYS AGO, BUT THAT'S WHERE ACCURATE SHOT LOGGING IS ESSENTIAL.

The same sort of confusion can arise with backgrounds and props. Was the blind up or down? Was the door to the outside loo closed or half-open?

Making sure that the details contained in each scene are kept consistent is known as 'continuity'. If you don't pay attention to it, your audience will notice your errors – and while they're thinking about this, they're not concentrating on the action or dialogue.

Continuity doesn't just apply to people, props and backgrounds. If one scene is supposed to directly follow another then care must be taken to ensure that the light and the background sounds are the same.

How to Control Continuity

It's very easy to lose track of continuity when you're filming your video out of sequence, but there are ways to keep a grip on things:

★ Storyboards: you can make notes on these as to what people were wearing, where they were looking, what they were doing etc.

★ Shot-lists: used in the same way as above.

★ Polaroid camera: great for taking a record of each scene. Puts an end to arguments such as 'I had my top button open', 'No you didn't', 'Yes I did', 'No I didn't!', 'Look, are you calling me a liar?' etc., etc.

★ Masking tape: little pieces on the floor can be used to mark people's positions between takes.

Special Hints

★Clocks: if these are in shot you'll need to adjust them so they show the passage of time accurately.

★Candles: remember, these burn down – never up! (The same rule applies to cigarettes.)

★Food: despite the story of the loaves and the fishes, a half-finished pizza on someone's plate cannot miraculously reconstitute itself into a whole one in a subsequent scene. (This applies to all food; there's nothing magical about pizzas.)

Who says that the professionals always get it right?

In *Captain Apache* (1971), the deputy sheriff is ambushed in the street and shot twice. He stumbles back into his office and falls down dead – with a knife in his chest.

In *Mary Poppins* (1964), her gloves change from white to black and back to white – all while reading a letter.

In *Duel* (1971), Dennis Weaver stops at a roadside grill and drinks a whole glass of water. He puts the glass down on the table and it's full up.

In *Days of Thunder* (1990), Tom Cruise injures his eye, resulting in a red ring around his eyeball. This starts on his left eye – then moves to his right.

In *An American in Paris* (1951), Gene Kelly sets out with eight paintings and manages to sell two of them – yet still comes back with eight.

In *1984* (1984), Richard Burton removes one of John Hurt's front teeth with pliers. A short while later it's miraculously grown back.

Shedding Light on Lighting

When it comes down to it, light is a heavy subject. There are so many aspects to take in but I'm not going to get all technical. Stuff like light levels in terms of lux and the temperature of light are for egg heads. And as for features like Automatic White Balance Controls, you can read about them in your camcorder handbook. What's more important is that you understand how light can affect what you're filming and how to compensate for it.

So, without further ado, settle down with a nice cup of Ovaltine and prepare to be illuminated . . .

Indoor Lighting

The performance of today's camcorders means that you don't need to spend a fortune on lighting equipment to get good results indoors – just removing lampshades and upgrading domestic lamps to 100W or 150W can really brighten a scene at little cost. Always remember that these bulbs get very, very hot.

You could even try re-positioning standard or table lamps to get a better or brighter spread of light. Nine times out of ten just upgrading light bulbs and moving lamps around will be sufficient to film indoors without any extra lighting. (It also keeps the setting 'informal' and makes people less conscious of the camcorder.)

If you find you do need extra lighting then consider these three options:

Beadle Tip

IF BUDGETS ARE REALLY TIGHT I ALWAYS TELL FRIENDS MOVING INTO NEW FLATS OR HOUSES TO SPEND THEIR MONEY ON LIGHTING RATHER THAN REDECORATION. YOU CAN CREATE COUNTLESS TYPES OF MOODS WITH GOOD LIGHTING. IT'S CHEAPER, EASIER AND MUCH MORE VERSATILE THAN CHANGING WALLPAPER OR CURTAINS.

Option 1: Improvised video lighting

★Low voltage domestic track lighting can be turned into an effective, portable lighting rig by using uprated spotlights (mount the track and transformer on a length of wood so it becomes easy to position).

★Similarly, a higher wattage bulb in an ordinary anglepoise desk lamp can also provide a useful, flexible light source.

★ You can also adapt exterior domestic security lights (the types found on patios) for interior use by mounting them on a simple stand and overriding (or not using) the infra-red sensor.

Option 2: Camera-mounted halogen lights

These mount on the top of the camera and might be mains or battery-powered. They're convenient but of limited use. They get very hot, they don't have much range and what they do light looks stark and bleached out (as you can tell, I'm not a great fan of them).

Option 3: Free-standing video lamps

The most popular and by far the most useful specialist video lights are free-standing Quartz Halogen units, usually rated at between 500W and 1000W. Some have large metal flaps around the front of the lamp (called 'barn doors') which can be opened or closed to change the spread of light from a wide floodlight to a tight spotlight.

Other lamps are Photofloods, a much cheaper (and less powerful) lamp used by stills photographers that give a softer, more diffused light.

Lighting Set-Ups

When filming interiors, lighting can make or break the mood. A soft, warm light creates a serene, mellow atmosphere, whereas subdued lighting with large areas in shadow suggests suspense – and something nasty about to happen. These are two extremes and you can use lighting to achieve hundreds of other effects.

Most artificial lighting set-ups consist of what's called the 'Three Point Method' – using a key light, a fill-in light and a backlight. It's known poshly as the 'Three Light Protocol', which sounds a bit like a Len Deighton novel (but isn't).

Key light

The main light. Positioned high up, to the front of and at 45° to your main subject. This light will naturally cast shadows across one side of your subject, which is why we need the . . .

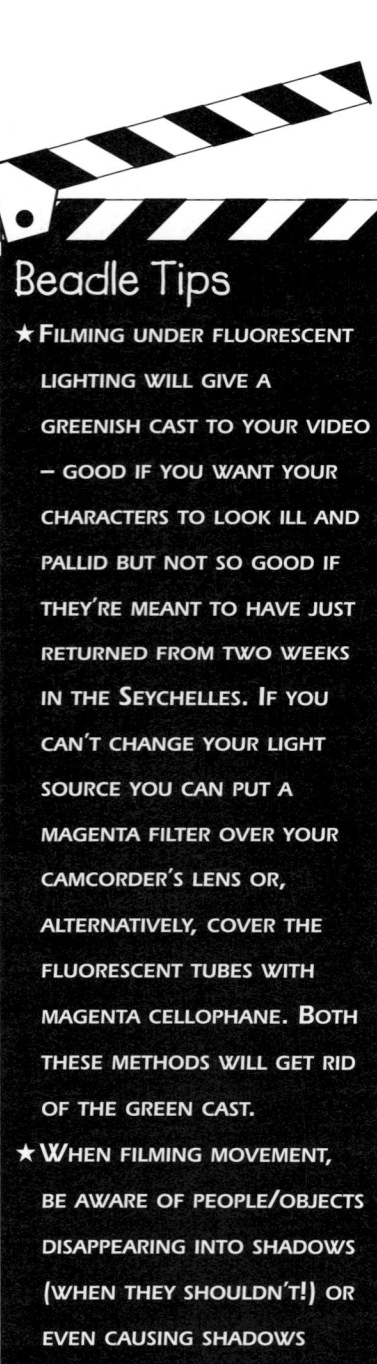

Beadle Tips

★ FILMING UNDER FLUORESCENT LIGHTING WILL GIVE A GREENISH CAST TO YOUR VIDEO – GOOD IF YOU WANT YOUR CHARACTERS TO LOOK ILL AND PALLID BUT NOT SO GOOD IF THEY'RE MEANT TO HAVE JUST RETURNED FROM TWO WEEKS IN THE SEYCHELLES. IF YOU CAN'T CHANGE YOUR LIGHT SOURCE YOU CAN PUT A MAGENTA FILTER OVER YOUR CAMCORDER'S LENS OR, ALTERNATIVELY, COVER THE FLUORESCENT TUBES WITH MAGENTA CELLOPHANE. BOTH THESE METHODS WILL GET RID OF THE GREEN CAST.

★ WHEN FILMING MOVEMENT, BE AWARE OF PEOPLE/OBJECTS DISAPPEARING INTO SHADOWS (WHEN THEY SHOULDN'T!) OR EVEN CAUSING SHADOWS INADVERTENTLY.

Fill-in light (or filler light)

This should be half the brightness of the key light and positioned lower down, closer to the subject but on the opposite side. This will lighten the areas in the shadows caused by the key light.

Backlight

This should be high, behind and to the side of your subject. It is used to cast highlights on your subject and separate them from the background.

An additional *background light* is sometimes used, pointing towards the background to help give an impression of depth to the shot and get rid of any shadows cast by the key and fill-in lights.

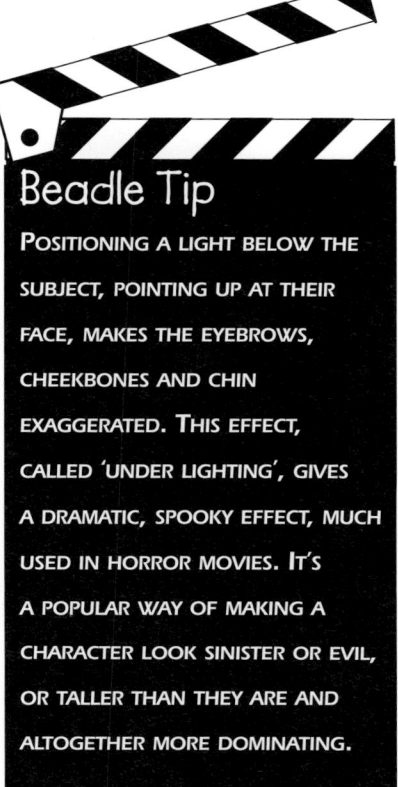

Beadle Tip

POSITIONING A LIGHT BELOW THE SUBJECT, POINTING UP AT THEIR FACE, MAKES THE EYEBROWS, CHEEKBONES AND CHIN EXAGGERATED. THIS EFFECT, CALLED 'UNDER LIGHTING', GIVES A DRAMATIC, SPOOKY EFFECT, MUCH USED IN HORROR MOVIES. IT'S A POPULAR WAY OF MAKING A CHARACTER LOOK SINISTER OR EVIL, OR TALLER THAN THEY ARE AND ALTOGETHER MORE DOMINATING.

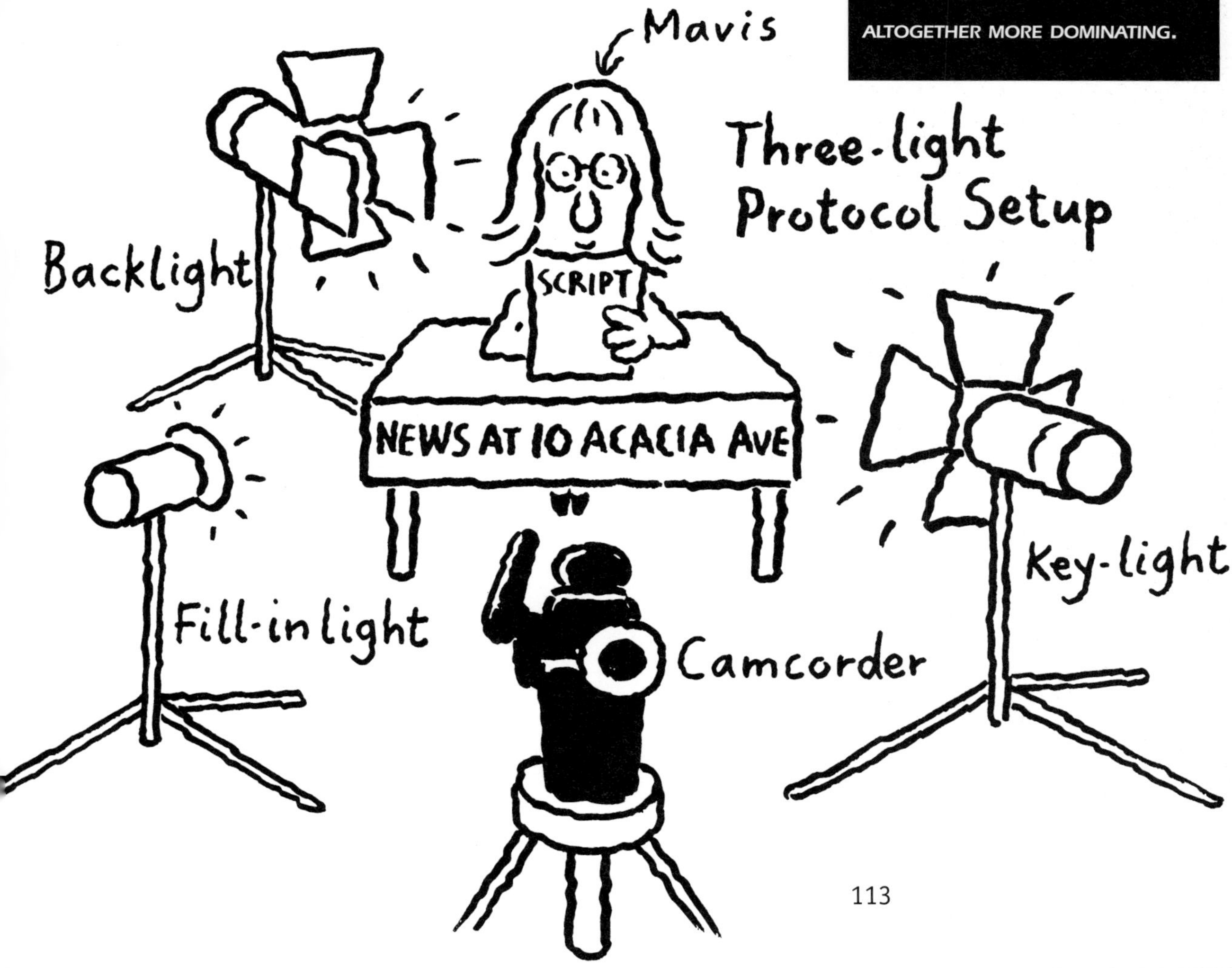

Mavis

Three-light Protocol Setup

Backlight

SCRIPT

NEWS AT 10 ACACIA AVE

Fill-in light

Camcorder

Key-light

113

Lighting Accessories

Reflectors

These are used indoors or outside to reflect artificial or natural light to give a more even spread of light and to help lighten areas in shadow. You can make them easily and cheaply by using large pieces of polystyrene. Alternatively, make a wooden framework and stretch a clean white sheet over it.

Covering your reflector with gold foil can add warmth to a shot, especially skin tones. (Flat foil gives a very pronounced reflection, while crumpling the foil before sticking it on will tend to give a more diffused effect.)

Diffusers

These are used to reduce the amount of light from a given source and can be made from any translucent material, like gauze or tracing paper, fixed to a framework. Moving them nearer or further away from the light will affect how bright it is – but be careful of the hot bulb. You don't want to find yourself filming a version of *London's Burning*.

Outdoor Lighting

You might think the best possible place to film is outdoors. After all, there's loads of light, it's free – and there are no cables to trip over.

Wrong! There is loads of light, but the biggest problem is that you can't control it. Bright sunshine gives far too much contrast; light areas can be too bright while areas in shadow can virtually disappear. Overcast days give a scene a dull, flat, lifeless look. You need shadows to add depth to your video, but the problem is how to control them. The answer is in manipulating the natural light by one of two methods:

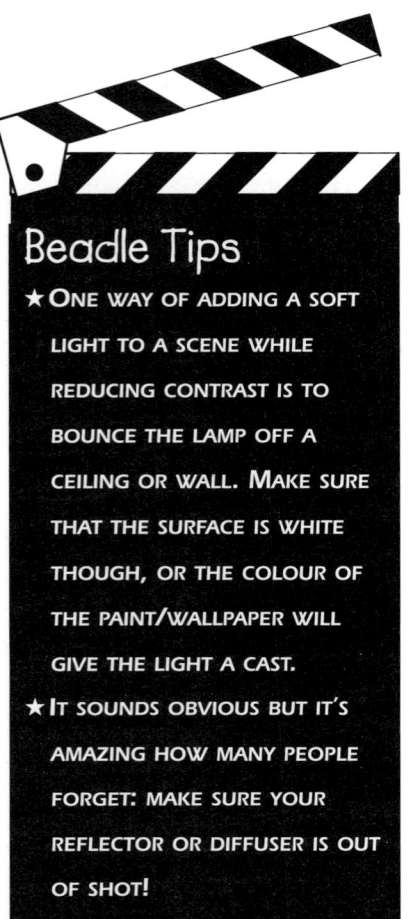

Beadle Tips

★ ONE WAY OF ADDING A SOFT LIGHT TO A SCENE WHILE REDUCING CONTRAST IS TO BOUNCE THE LAMP OFF A CEILING OR WALL. MAKE SURE THAT THE SURFACE IS WHITE THOUGH, OR THE COLOUR OF THE PAINT/WALLPAPER WILL GIVE THE LIGHT A CAST.

★ IT SOUNDS OBVIOUS BUT IT'S AMAZING HOW MANY PEOPLE FORGET: MAKE SURE YOUR REFLECTOR OR DIFFUSER IS OUT OF SHOT!

1: Adding light to parts of the scene in shadow

If you don't want to, or can't, use artificial lights, a reflector will enable you to shoot in the shade by reflecting natural light back at the subject to add detail. Filming someone near a building with a bright wall, for example, will have the same effect.

2: Reducing light to parts of the scene in sunlight

The simplest method is to move your subject into the shade, and use a reflector to open up some of the detail that is lost. You can also use a large diffuser to reduce the amount of bright sunlight reaching your subject in this way.

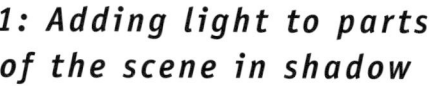

Beadle Tips

WHEN FILMING OUTDOORS:

★ AVOID FILMING EITHER WITH THE SUN DIRECTLY BEHIND OR OVERHEAD. IF YOU DO EITHER OF THESE, YOUR SUBJECT WILL LOOK FLAT, UNINTERESTING AND WILL PROBABLY BE STRAINING AGAINST THE LIGHT TO SEE (OK IF YOU'RE FILMING 'THE INCREDIBLE SQUINTING MAN' BUT NOT THAT GOOD FOR MOST OTHER THINGS).

★ SHORT SHADOWS ON YOUR SUBJECT WILL ADD DEPTH TO YOUR PICTURE.

★ AVOID SHOOTING INTO THE SUN UNLESS YOU REALLY WANT TO END UP WITH A SILHOUETTE.

★ THE BEST TIMES TO FILM ARE THE EARLY MORNINGS OR AFTER IT'S BEEN RAINING. AT THESE TIMES THE AIR'S CLEARER AND THE LIGHT TENDS TO BE 'CLEANER'.

Stunts

The first rule of stunts for the amateur film maker is 'Never do any stunts'. There are people who get paid vast sums of money in Hollywood to do what you see in the movies. They train for years. They have every conceivable safety back-up. And there's still few of them who haven't broken nearly every bone in their body at some time or another. Be sensible.

When you're filming, never do anything remotely dangerous. Ever. Making a Blockbuster is about having fun, not putting people's lives at risk to get that one special effects shot. It isn't worth it and if you kill all your friends you'll have no one to star in your next epic.

Falls

The most common risk camcorder users take is with heights and falls. Even a short fall can be risky. Cheat the shot.

★Shoot a shot of your character about to jump. Don't put them on a roof top. Instead, crouch down on the ground so that you're filming looking up at them against the sky. Have them tensed, as if to jump.

★Perhaps go to a cut-away of someone looking up at them.

★Have your character jump up, right out of frame.

★Set your camcorder up ready for a close-up of your character's feet on the ground. Have them jump in the air and record their feet as they land.

★To complete the illusion, have them look back up at the place they're supposed to have jumped from.

If you want a point-of-view shot of someone plunging from a height, go up to the place they're supposed to fall from – provided it's safe – film down towards the ground and do a fast zoom in. Dub on a shout or a scream later.

Beadle Tip

IT'S EASY TO GET CARRIED AWAY WHEN YOU WANT TO GET THAT EXTRA-SPECIAL SHOT, BUT YOU KNOW YOU'VE GONE TOO FAR WHEN YOU HEAR YOURSELF SAYING SOMETHING LIKE:

★'SO YOU HANG THERE. THEN YOU LET GO, DROP, TWIST TO AVOID THE RAILINGS AND LAND HERE . . .'

★'AT THIS POINT, TONY SMEARS YOU WITH A LIBERAL COATING OF LIGHTER FLUID . . .'

★'FIONA COMES AT YOU WITH THE CARVING KNIFE, BUT YOU TWIST ASIDE AT THE LAST MOMENT . . .'

★'GO ON, GRANDAD – YOU CAN JUMP THAT!'

Water

The great comedian W.C. Fields used to say he avoided water because 'fish have sex in it' – but there are other equally good reasons to steer well clear.

You can never trust a stretch of river or canal, or a lake or filled-in gravel pit. There can be all kinds of underwater currents you can't see and obstructions like pieces of junk or weeds just waiting to trap the unwary. Being a strong swimmer is no guarantee of safety, and you can drown in very shallow water.

The most sensible option is not to write a script which calls for anyone to fall into water. If you have to do it, again, cheat. Film your character beside the river, stream etc., then cut to a series of very tight close-ups filmed with your character lying inside a children's paddling pool or a bath tub – a partially submerged face, hands thrashing etc. You can cut-away to reactions from people standing on the bank to maintain the illusion.

Fire

If you play with fire, you're going to get burned. Even controlled fires have a habit of suddenly flaring up and catching alight everything in the vicinity. If you don't believe me, ask your local fire brigade how many garden sheds they've had to extinguish this year already, because someone's bonfire grew out of control.

Fire doesn't even look good on video either. The intensity of the flames tends to burn an image on to your lens and can leave an ugly 'after-smear' on the tape for several seconds afterwards.

If at all possible, avoid fire in your scripts. If you absolutely have to use it, there are some safe ways of creating a fire effect. Magic dealers sell very safe pyro devices like flash cotton and flash paper – but remember to read the instructions!

Special Effects

You can fill a book with special effects hints and tips. Some people already have. If you really want to know more about the 'tricks of the trade', read them.

Here, I'd just like to run you through some of the most basic special effects – camera tricks, filters and special effects make-up.

Day for Night

So, you're filming a spooky thriller. The action takes place at night in a deserted cemetery – but there are a few problems. Your cast and crew prefer to sleep at night. They don't want to go into a cemetery in the dead of night, thank you very much. Anyway, the cemetery won't give you permission to film at night – and your camcorder's no good at night either.

So what do you do? Well, either you change your title to 'The Ghoul Who Walked by Day' or you cheat.

'Day for Night' is the technical term for filming night-time scenes during the day. It's perfectly possible, using a few tricks of the trade and a filter:

★If your camcorder permits it, change the White Balance on your camcorder to the indoor light setting – even though you're filming outside (refer to your camcorder's handbook).

★If you have a manual exposure facility, turn it down just a tad so that the picture is slightly under-exposed.

★Now screw a dark-blue colour filter over your lens to darken your picture.

★Lastly, ignore all sensible advice and shoot the action towards the sun instead of with the sun behind you. This improves the contrast in the picture and the sun will look like the moon. (Don't point the camera directly at the sun however!)

The Disappearing Act

A good ghost can just disappear into thin air right in front of your eyes. This effect is quite easy to achieve on video, without any need for wires, mirrors or supernatural intervention – but it can look super!

Here's how you do it:

★ Set your camcorder firmly on a tripod so it can't move.

★ Shoot normally until the ghost is due to disappear. Make sure that no one is moving, except possibly the ghost.

★ Put your camera on pause. (NB If your camcorder has a remote control facility use it to avoid even the slightest camera movement.)

★ Make sure everything – and everybody – in the frame keeps perfectly still as the 'ghost' walks out of the frame.

★ Turn 'pause' off and resume filming.

You can also use this effect to 'teleport' science fiction characters or to have people magically change their clothes, grow longer hair, age etc.

Evil Shape-Changers

You can achieve Jekyll and Hyde type transformations on camera without any special equipment. Try it – but use a tripod.

★ Switch your camcorder to manual focus.

★ Frame your beautiful heroine as a medium close-up and make sure she keeps still.

★ The camcorder should be absolutely still as well.

★ Use your manual focus to blur her image until she's just an unrecognisable smear.

★ Press pause on your camcorder (again, use a remote control facility if you have one).

★ Remove your heroine and put an ugly, horrible monster in her exact place.

★ Turn the camcorder on to record again.

★ Re-adjust the manual focus until the monster is sharp.

For the best effect, dub some spooky music over the transformation later!

Special Effects Filters

There are countless filters available for camcorders including those that can turn points of light into star bursts, create a fog effect, give the picture an old-time sepia look, change the colour of the sky or make multiple images of a subject (great for monster movie point-of-view shots!). Your camcorder dealer probably stocks the filters and the filter holder that attaches to your lens. If he doesn't, tell him he should.

Pure Magic!

Many of the special effects props you need are easily available – because they're really magic tricks. Whether it's a trick knife or a plate that moves by itself, you'll find the perfect equipment at a novelty or magic shop. Look for them in your local *Yellow Pages*.

Novelty shops are ideal for simple, cheap and cheerful gag props, funny masks and so on. Magic shops are much more serious affairs. These people are usually experts. Tell them what you want to do and chances are they'll be able to suggest ten different ways in which you can do it!

If you're not a member of the Magic Circle, don't expect them to tell you how the illusions or tricks are created. They'll demonstrate them for you – if you decide to buy – then you get to find out how they work. Once you see how it's done, you'll often be staggered at the sheer simplicity – but you'd never have guessed!

Magic stores are great for safe pyro (fire) tricks, little explosive devices called Bingos (which are spring loaded percussion caps) and ultra-thin almost totally invisible wires you can use to make objects move by themselves. Visit one. You'll come out full of great ideas – and maybe even with a new hobby!

Make-Up Hints and Tips

It's beyond the scope of this book to go into detail about how to achieve every type of make-up effect – monster, zombie, accident victim, person from the future, silent movie star, old person, half-man-half-biscuit etc., etc. The best thing to do is consult a stage make-up book, or one of the many books now available for children's face painting.

Beadle Tip

TO GIVE A SHOT A ROMANTIC, SOFT FOCUS EFFECT, SMEAR A LITTLE VASELINE ON TO A CLEAR FILTER IN FRONT OF YOUR LENS. NEVER APPLY VASELINE TO THE CAMERA LENS ITSELF! ANOTHER TRICK IS TO STRETCH FINE-MESH NYLON STOCKINGS OVER THE LENS TO CREATE THE SAME EFFECT.

Beadle's 'Did You Know?'

IN STAR TREK, THE GLITTERING EFFECT SEEN AS THE TRANSPORTER DISSOLVED AND THEN RE-ENERGISED PEOPLE'S ATOMS WAS ACHIEVED BY STAGE HANDS THROWING HANDFULS OF ALUMINIUM DUST INTO AN EXTREMELY BRIGHT VERTICAL BEAM OF LIGHT.

Turn your child into a puppy with face paints (just make sure she's house-trained)

Aliens/Monsters - Some Special Tips

★Nose putty can be used to change the shape of your nose but you can also use it to add an extra nose. Or two extra ones, for that matter. For all we know, the inhabitants of Rigel IV might have three noses (mind you, I pity them if they catch a cold).

★You can use it in the same way to add or modify any other features. Maybe you need Mr Spock ears, small horns protruding from your forehead, a wart the size of a champagne cork - even a third nipple.

★Scales or similar can be made simply by cutting out small pieces of gauze and applying them to the skin, then covering them with make-up.

★Aerosol metallic face paints are useful for turning people into robots.

Blood, Blood, Glorious Blood

You can buy fake blood in bottles or capsules.

To simulate a wound:

Take some liquid blood and seal it in a small bag made from cellophane or cling-film. This should then be attached to the appropriate part of the body with plasters and hidden under light-coloured clothing. To make the blood flow your victim should clutch at the wound, piercing the bag with a pin concealed in his or her hand.

To simulate blood dripping from the mouth:

Keep a blood capsule hidden in your cheeks and bite it at the appropriate moment (NB Although harmless, the blood in blood capsules does taste a bit odd. Make sure your performers get used to it before filming for real. A vampire who winces and says 'Yukkkk!' when biting a virgin's neck will not be that convincing).

Beadle's 'Did You Know?'

'THAT SCENE'

ONE OF THE MOST FAMOUS SCENES IN MOVIE HISTORY IS THE 'SHOWER' SCENE FROM ALFRED HITCHCOCK'S *PSYCHO*. IT'S JUST 45 SECONDS LONG BUT TOOK SEVEN DAYS TO GET RIGHT. THE MOST DIFFICULT SHOT WAS THE CLOSE-UP OF JANET LEIGH'S EYES AS SHE LIES DEAD ON THE FLOOR NEXT TO THE SHOWER. IT'S A LONG SCENE AND THE TROUBLE WAS MAKING SURE JANET LEIGH DIDN'T BLINK (WELL, NOT MANY DEAD PEOPLE BLINK, DO THEY?). HITCHCOCK RACKED HIS BRAINS FOR A SOLUTION AND IN THE END HE CHEATED! HE USED THREE DIFFERENT SHOTS: ONE OF JANET LEIGH STARING WIDE-EYED, DESPERATELY TRYING NOT TO BLINK, A CLOSE UP OF THE SHOWER HEAD AND A STILL PHOTOGRAPH OF JANET'S EYES.

BY CUTTING FROM THE STILL PHOTO TO THE SHOWER HEAD AND THEN THE SHOT OF THE 'REAL' JANET LEIGH, HE TRICKED AUDIENCES INTO BELIEVING THAT JANET LEIGH AVOIDED BLINKING FOR AN INCREDIBLE LENGTH OF TIME - A GREAT EXAMPLE OF INGENUITY AT WORK. (NOW YOU KNOW, YOU CAN HAVE A GO!)

OH YES, ONE OTHER FACT FOR TRIVIA FANS: THE BLOOD SEEN DRAINING AWAY IN THE SHOWER WAS ACTUALLY CHOCOLATE SAUCE (REMEMBER, IT WAS A BLACK AND WHITE FILM).

Prompt Cards - the Amateur's Autocue

If your cast are the sort of people who have trouble remembering where they left their car keys then don't leave it to chance when it comes to getting them to remember lines.

Imagine the scene - you've got the lighting and sound just right, two other actors have delivered performances worthy of an Oscar and it's time for Uncle Clive to deliver the funniest punchline in the history of comedy. But he can't. He knows it's something about a baboon. Or was it a monsoon? Then again, he's pretty sure it involved a lagoon.

It might be funny at the time - but it won't be after the fifteenth take.

So what's the solution? Well, the answer's written on the cards. Prompt cards. These are simply large cards (I find that 30" x 20" is best) on which the script, or preferably just key words, are written in marker pen as an *aide-mémoire*.

An alternative to using prompt cards is to write lines of dialogue on small labels which you can attach to anywhere out of shot, e.g. on a table top, inside a book, on a photo frame -

even inside your palm. The idea isn't to read from them - they're just there to remind you of your lines before you have to say them.

Left: Rehearsing a key scene in 'Pocket Money is Forever'

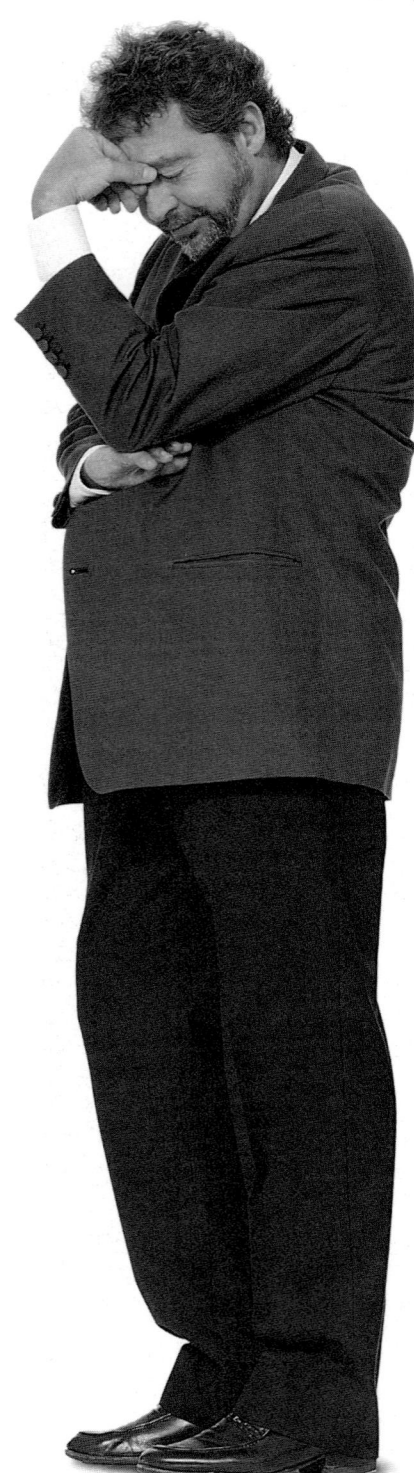

Sound Effects

It's amazing how many different (and authentic-sounding) effects can be made using just your imagination and some common household objects. Orson Welles made the sound of the hatch unscrewing on the Martian spacecraft, in the 1936 radio play *War of the Worlds*, by slowly unscrewing the lid of a coffee jar while holding it in a toilet bowl to give an eerie, echoey metallic effect.

Moving a microphone nearer or further away can often give quite different variations.

DIY Sound Effects

Thunder: blow gently across the top of a microphone or wobble something like a biscuit tin lid or a baking tray.

Breaking glass: although you can smash an old bottle or pane of glass in a cardboard box (be careful!), you can also get the same sort of noise by dropping pieces of thick metal on to a hard surface or by shaking cutlery in a biscuit tin.

Car crash: get an assortment of nuts and bolts, small pieces of metal and some glass and experiment with dropping the whole lot on to different surfaces (with care!).

Horses: you can't beat half-coconut shells knocked together – or hitting a table top with two upside-down plastic cups. Drumming your fingers or fingertips on a table top also sounds good and you can vary the intensity to simulate horses coming closer/going further away.

Tramping through thick snow: walk on the spot in a large box that's been filled with polystyrene packaging, shredded paper – or loads of old video tape. Alternatively, squeeze a half-empty bag of flour.

Geiger counter: hold four or five pens or pencils of similar size in a row in one hand, then rub the point of another pen or pencil across them to make a clicking sound. The further away, the more sporadic the clicking, then build up a crescendo of clicks until you're supposedly standing on a plutonium fuel rod.

Foghorn: blow gently across the top of a bottle half-filled with water. Changing the amount of water will change the tone of the foghorn.

Jet engine: use a vacuum cleaner.

Train: rub two pieces of sandpaper together.

Crackling fire: crumple up a piece of cellophane or heavy brown paper.

Rain: pour salt or sugar slowly down a tube made of rolled-up paper. Alternatively, roll peas slowly around on a metal tray or pour them into a sieve that's held above the microphone. Another method is to drop grains of rice slowly on to a piece of greaseproof paper that's been stretched over a tin can and held in place by an elastic band.

Creaking doors: slowly pull your (dry) fingers across an inflated balloon.

Pneumatic doors (the type that no inter-galactic spacecraft would be without): a bicycle or car pump will give the necessary 'hiss'. Experiment with holding your finger over the end of the nozzle to vary the sound. (NB Be careful when you do this. Super hi-tech doors are not known for making a 'farty' sound when they open or close.)

Someone talking on the telephone: speak into a headphone that's been plugged into the microphone socket of your tape recorder. (Alternatively, just record someone saying their lines over a telephone!)

Rustling trees: scrunch up cassette tape.

The wind: pull silk or thin paper across the sharp edge of a table (with a side-to-side motion).

Knife wound: slashing a cabbage with a real knife gives a realistic stabbing effect – just be very careful with the knife!

Gun shots: burst a balloon with a pin.

Bubbling liquids in a laboratory: blow into a bowl of water with a straw.

Monsters: the purr of a moggie, when recorded close-up, can sound like a much larger beast.

Of course, one way to obtain common sound effects is to record them yourself, using an extension microphone. If you want a really good sound of a door being unbolted, record a real door being unbolted. If you want a creaky floorboard, record a real creaky floorboard. Simple!

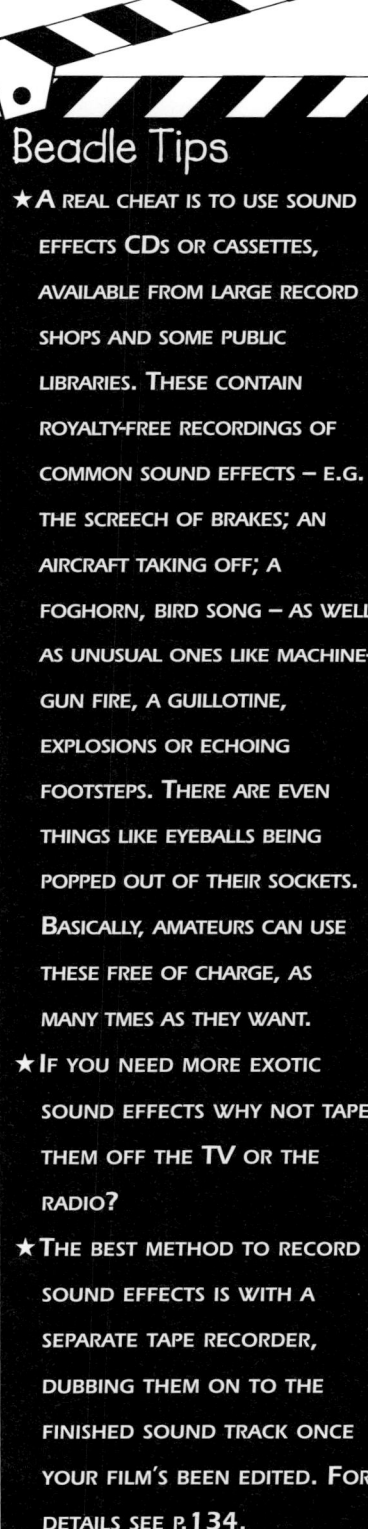

Beadle Tips

★ A REAL CHEAT IS TO USE SOUND EFFECTS CDs OR CASSETTES, AVAILABLE FROM LARGE RECORD SHOPS AND SOME PUBLIC LIBRARIES. THESE CONTAIN ROYALTY-FREE RECORDINGS OF COMMON SOUND EFFECTS – E.G. THE SCREECH OF BRAKES; AN AIRCRAFT TAKING OFF; A FOGHORN, BIRD SONG – AS WELL AS UNUSUAL ONES LIKE MACHINE-GUN FIRE, A GUILLOTINE, EXPLOSIONS OR ECHOING FOOTSTEPS. THERE ARE EVEN THINGS LIKE EYEBALLS BEING POPPED OUT OF THEIR SOCKETS. BASICALLY, AMATEURS CAN USE THESE FREE OF CHARGE, AS MANY TMES AS THEY WANT.

★ IF YOU NEED MORE EXOTIC SOUND EFFECTS WHY NOT TAPE THEM OFF THE TV OR THE RADIO?

★ THE BEST METHOD TO RECORD SOUND EFFECTS IS WITH A SEPARATE TAPE RECORDER, DUBBING THEM ON TO THE FINISHED SOUND TRACK ONCE YOUR FILM'S BEEN EDITED. FOR DETAILS SEE P.134.

Sound Advice on Sound Recording

Your sound quality is more important than your shot quality. You might think that sounds like a rash statement but trust Beadle.

People will forgive a shot that's slightly too dark or one that's framed badly. They will even forgive poor direction or a bad edit (if they even notice it), but the one thing they will not forgive is poor sound. If it's too loud, it becomes muffled. If it's too quiet, then the tape hiss is intrusive (all tapes give hiss at low volumes – you can't avoid it). Worse still, if it's indistinct, then Heaven help you.

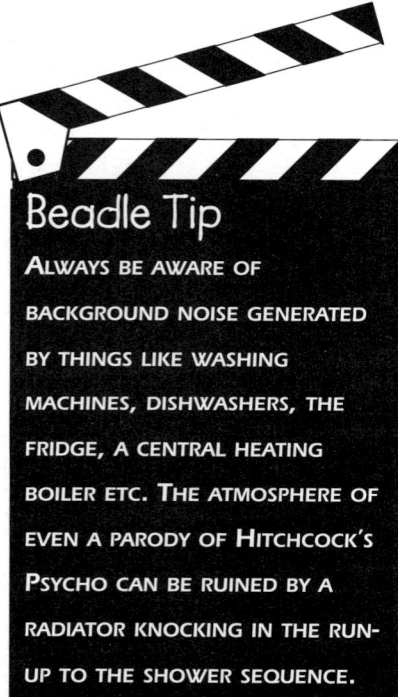

Beadle Tip

ALWAYS BE AWARE OF BACKGROUND NOISE GENERATED BY THINGS LIKE WASHING MACHINES, DISHWASHERS, THE FRIDGE, A CENTRAL HEATING BOILER ETC. THE ATMOSPHERE OF EVEN A PARODY OF HITCHCOCK'S PSYCHO CAN BE RUINED BY A RADIATOR KNOCKING IN THE RUN-UP TO THE SHOWER SEQUENCE.

The Problem

I always advise budding video makers that if they're working to a tight budget (which they always are), to invest money in improving their sound equipment. The standard microphones built in to camcorders are OK but they're not very good at discriminating between sounds – someone talking, the traffic, ambient noise – treating each sound they pick up as being equally important.

The Solution!

The answer is an external or 'off-camera' microphone – of which there are loads to choose from, each with different characteristics. These all plug straight into the socket marked 'Extension Mic' or 'Ext Mic' (although not all camcorders have this facility). They can be mounted directly on to the camcorder via a bracket (keeping it away from the noise of the zooming motor) – or, better still, held out of shot on a long pole, or 'boom' as it's known, and connected to the camera by a lead. Let's have a look at a few types of external microphones:

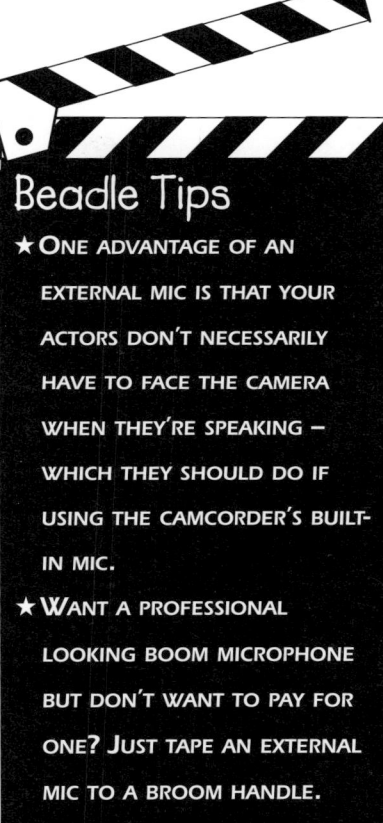

Omnidirectional mics

This type of microphone is the one that's usually built in to the camcorder. They're designed to pick up sound equally from all directions. Useful for capturing ambient sounds or a group of people talking, but not good for picking out individuals.

Unidirectional mics

These pick up sounds mainly from the direction they're pointing in and are used to record one person talking or specific noises. (Real clever clogs also know these as Cardioid mics – but they're just showing off.)

Tie-clip mics

These omnidirectional or unidirectional tie-clip mics are the best way of getting a microphone close to the subject you're taping. They're very easy to conceal, but make sure the wearer is aware of the mic at all times. Accidentally knocking it – or even touching it with clothing – will cause horrible 'popping' and other unwanted sounds.

Radio-mics (or 'wireless mics')

These get round the problem of trying to hide cables but unless you can afford a really professional (i.e. expensive) one, don't bother. Cheap ones are more trouble than they're worth. They can pick up interference from nearby car engines, the metal framework of a building – even rogue mini-cab transmissions.

Always use headphones to monitor sound

Using a specialised external mic is all well and good, but you have to make sure you know what sounds it's actually picking up (or even if it's working at all). For this you have to monitor your sound recording via a pair of headphones. These plug into the socket marked 'Headphone' or just 'Phone'. It's best to use headphones that enclose the ears fully. Yes, they're heavy and make your ears really sweaty, but they screen all extraneous sounds so you can be sure that what you hear is what the microphone is actually picking up.

Personal-stereo-type headphones, while OK, allow you to hear other noises which can be distracting and give you a false indication of what's being recorded.

Beadle Tips

★ IT'S VERY DIFFICULT TO FIND A DAY WHEN THE AIR IS PERFECTLY STILL. THE SLIGHTEST BREEZE CAN SOUND LIKE A HURRICANE IF IT HITS THE MICROPHONE DIRECTLY. HOWEVER, A WAY ROUND THIS IS TO COVER THE MIC WITH A WIND-SHIELD OR WIND-SOCK, WHICH IS USUALLY MADE FROM POROUS FOAM RUBBER OR A FURRY MATERIAL WHICH SLIDES OVER THE MIC ITSELF (MAKING YOUR CAMCORDER LOOK LIKE IT'S MATING WITH SOME SORT OF SMALL MARSUPIAL).

★ IF YOU'RE RECORDING AN INTERVIEW USING A HAND HELD MICROPHONE, BE CONSCIOUS OF RINGS WORN ON FINGERS. THESE CAN KNOCK AGAINST THE BODY OF THE MICROPHONE, CREATING A LOUD TAPPING SOUND.

Titles and Credits – The Finishing Touch

Every Blockbuster should have credits. It should open with the title and close with a full credit list of everyone involved.

If you don't own a camcorder with a built-in character generator – or a flashy processor – there are still plenty of different low-cost ways you can make your credits.

★ Sheets of Letraset rub-down transfer letters are available from stationers in a wide variety of typefaces. Line the letters up using faint pencil rules. It's harder than it looks, but it can give a very professional effect.

★ Most word processing programmes on home PCs give you the option to blow words up, make them bold and to put them in different typefaces. You can use these to make stylish credits.

★ Print your credits by hand on some big sheets of paper and video them. You can buy letter stencils from most good stationers if your handwriting's atrocious!

★ Do a Bob Dylan. Remember his video for 'Subterranean Homesick Blues' where he stands in front of the camera and holds up a series of caption boards?

★ Use Scrabble squares.

★ Announce the credits yourself as a voiceover over short clips from the Blockbuster, or over stills you've taken in production and then videoed.

★ Write letters in chalk on a children's blackboard.

★ Film each member of the cast and crew and get them to recite their role in the Blockbuster.

★ Did your Blockbuster star your children? Why not get them to write the credits in big letters and in bright colours on a series of sheets of paper – and then film the sheets? If they're too young to write, why not spell out the credits with their building blocks!

Beadle Tips

★ ALLOW PEOPLE TIME TO READ YOUR CAPTIONS. KEEP EACH NAME ON SCREEN FOR A GOOD 2 TO 3 SECONDS AT LEAST. NEVER HAVE MORE THAN SIX LINES OF TEXT ON SCREEN AT ONE TIME.

★ MAKE YOUR CREDIT SHEETS LOOK MORE INTERESTING BY STICKING RELEVANT PICTURES FROM BOOKS OR MAGAZINES ON THEM.

★ IF YOU CAN, AVOID USING PURE WHITE PAPER FOR YOUR CREDITS. IT CAN APPEAR A BIT DAZZLING ON SCREEN. GO FOR OFF-WHITE OR A LIGHT GREY INSTEAD.

★ IF YOU CAN, MAKE YOUR TITLES IN THE STYLE THAT SUITS YOUR BLOCKBUSTER. USE WACKY LETTERS FOR A SCREWBALL COMEDY; LETTERS CUT OUT OF A NEWSPAPER FOR A COMEDY KIDNAP DRAMA AND SO ON.

Editing Your Blockbuster

This section isn't for those who have already done their editing in-camera, shooting all their shots in order, but for those who have plumped for the extra flexibility and polish allowed by editing afterwards – which is called 'assembly editing'.

Editing video is very different from editing film. With film, you literally cut and join strips of film together. With video, it's all done electronically, so put your scissors and sticky tape away now!

Beadle Tip

IF YOU FEEL YOU WANT TO PLAY AROUND WITH EDITING BEFORE YOU START THE REAL EDIT, TO GET A FEEL FOR HOW IT ALL WORKS, DON'T USE YOUR MASTER TAPE. TO SAVE WEAR AND TEAR, MAKE A COPY OF IT AND USE THIS FOR MUCKING ABOUT AND EXPERIMENTING. ONLY USE THE ORIGINAL TAPE WHEN YOU'RE FINALLY CONFIDENT AND READY TO START ON THE REAL EDIT. OH – AND ALWAYS TAKE THE TAB OUT OF YOUR MASTER TAPE TO STOP YOU ACCIDENTALLY RECORDING OVER ALL YOUR HARD WORK. DON'T SAY I DIDN'T WARN YOU!

To edit your Blockbuster, you have to copy the shots you want on to another tape, in the order you want them.

To do this you either connect your camcorder up to your VCR at home or – if you have a VHS-C camcorder – pop the tape with your shots on into a second VCR and connect those two machines up. You should also connect the VCR receiving the signal up to your TV set, so you can see what you're doing. Make sure that sound and picture are both coming through. You'll have to sort out what connecting leads you need yourself, because they vary so much and I don't know what equipment you've got!

Now you copy the shots you want over to a new cassette on the second machine in the order you want them, gradually building up your finished video one shot at a time.

After you've completed each edit, play it back and make sure you're happy with it. If you're not, go back and do it again. It's worth taking the time and trouble now to get just the result you want.

Editing can be fiddly at first – but persevere. Practise. Play around with it before you start properly. Doing a good job here will make your finished video 100% better!

The 'ins' and 'outs' of editing

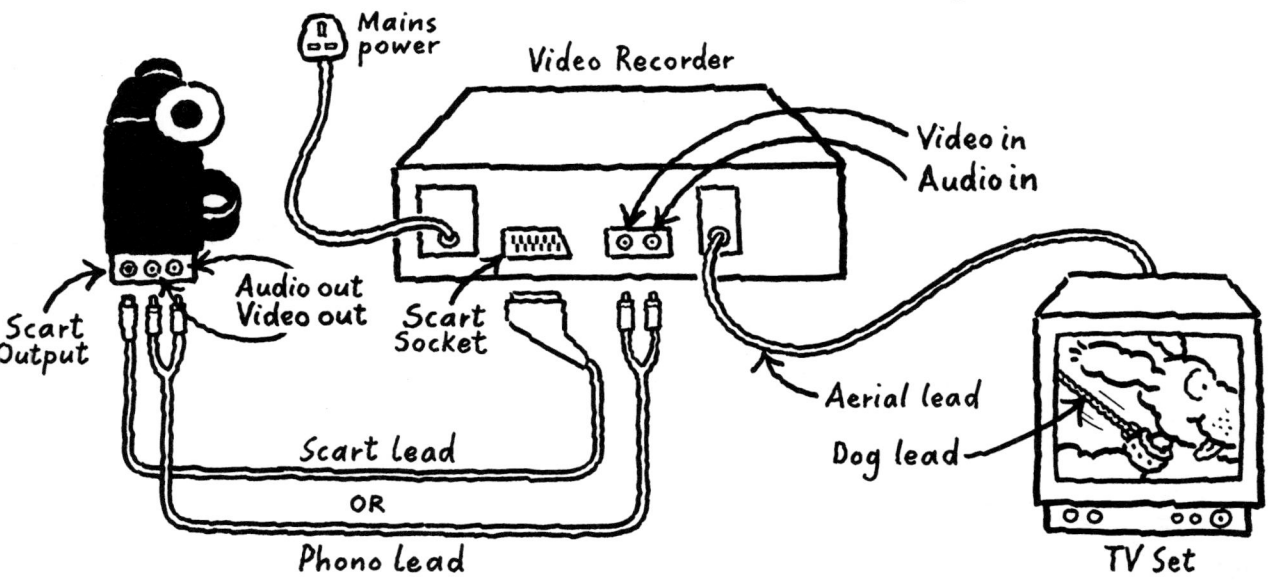

Editing with Your PC

With the right equipment and software, you can convert your video into a digital signal, ready for assembly in the order you want on your PC. You can dub it back on to video tape again (at the same time you can also add all sorts of special effects and titles).

Of course, with the new generation of digital camcorders now starting to appear on the shelves, this process will no doubt become simpler and simpler but – at the moment at least – this is still a highly complex area, full of compatibility questions. Special interface equipment and software is needed to get all the bits talking to one another. The best advice is to ask PC and camcorder dealers for guidance. Specialist stores are more likely to know than high street shops. Digital editing, whether in-camera or via PC, is the future.

The Art of Editing

You don't know this – but you've been to editing school all your life. You've seen literally millions of examples of every conceivable type of edit – because you've seen thousands and thousands of TV shows and feature films.

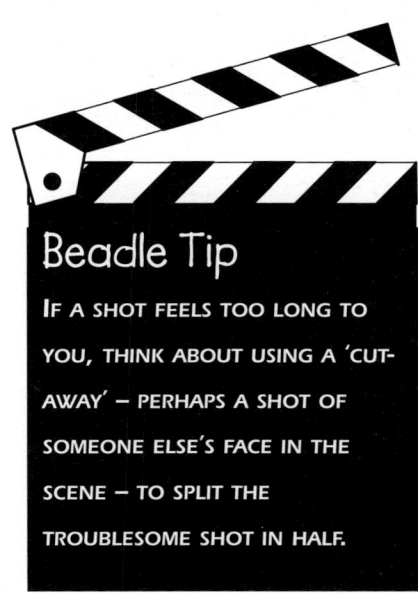

Beadle Tip

IF A SHOT FEELS TOO LONG TO YOU, THINK ABOUT USING A 'CUT-AWAY' – PERHAPS A SHOT OF SOMEONE ELSE'S FACE IN THE SCENE – TO SPLIT THE TROUBLESOME SHOT IN HALF.

You already know the secret rules of editing – at least subconsciously. Now all you have to do is apply them to your Blockbuster as you assemble it. Because of your vast experience, you should learn to trust your own judgement. If the edit looks right to you then it probably is. If it doesn't, then there's probably something wrong and you should do what you can to fix it.

Here's a handy reminder of the rules you already know, but don't realise you do . . .

The Secret Rules of Editing

★Don't hold on a shot too long. We discussed shot length earlier. Now, if you can, try to trim a second or two off in the edit. Lengthy shots look flabby and slow down the pace.

★Don't cut when someone's in mid-movement. The audience expects to see that movement completed. The exception to this rule is when the very next shot shows the movement completed, for example, when the first shot shows a punch being thrown and the very next shows it landing on some unfortunate.

★Use your editing to give you pace. The shorter the shot, the faster your video moves. However, this doesn't mean that you should string together a sequence of one-second shots! The human eye can't cope and Uncle Barry will probably have one of his 'turns' on the living room carpet.

★Don't cut when the camera is in the middle of a pan, track, zoom or tilt.

Don't Throw Away Your Out-Takes!

Remember that magic moment when your best friend Kathy was concentrating so hard on her role that she walked into a lamp post – or when Uncle Fred forgot his lines and let fly with a stream of obscenities that would make Liam Gallagher blush?

Don't throw them away!

Instead, you should edit them together and show them straight after your video. It's a great end to a screening! If you're going to be making captions, generate one that says 'Out-Takes' or

Beadle Tip

DON'T START EDITING UNTIL YOU'VE FINISHED SHOOTING THE ENTIRE PRODUCTION. LEAVING HOLES FOR SCENES WHICH STILL NEED SHOOTING IS A RECIPE FOR DISASTER. SUPPOSE YOUR MISSING SHOT TURNS OUT TO BE THREE SECONDS LONGER THAN THE TIME YOU'VE ALLOCATED FOR IT?

'Bloopers' or 'Never Work with Amateurs' to let your audience know what's coming.

Alternatively, you can make a mini-production of the whole thing. You could consider producing 'The Making of . . .' like all the big Hollywood blockbusters do these days. Cut your out-takes together with specially shot interviews with your cast and crew talking about your video and how it was made. Remember, this is their big chance to get back at you for all the bullying, whingeing, snapping and snarling you subjected them to during the production. Ask them leading questions like 'What did you think of the director?'

You could produce your own version of *It'll Be All Right on the Night.* Of course, you may be tempted to start this with the genuine opening titles recorded from the real show, but that's copyright material and

we know by now the rules about such things. To make it extra authentic, sit in a chair and start every sentence with: 'And if you're old enough to remember when . . .'

Left: How about using out-takes in your own version of You've Been Framed? *(If I ever find out who this is pretending to be me, I'll kill 'em!)*

Do not, under any circumstances, make your own version of *You've Been Framed* and do a cruel and heartless impersonation of me with a piece of bath mat glued to your face and a cushion stuck up your shirt.

Sound Editing

What you're about to read might be upsetting. No. I'm not going to tell you the truth about Father Christmas, or reveal what really happened to the *Blue Peter* pets when they got old – don't worry. I'm going to tell you that editing the sound on your video (or, as the process is known, 'dubbing') is quite complicated. Not only that, but you might not be able to do it.

It's not because you're dim and can't figure it out – but because the tape format you're using, your camcorder or your VCR might not allow this facility. Equally, you might not have access to a sound mixer – but don't worry. What's more important is that you understand the principles, so when you do feel a little more adventurous, you'll know what to do.

But Why Would I Want to Edit the Sound on My Video, Jeremy?

Good question. You might not want to. You might be so happy with your edited video that you'll watch it, fold your arms across your chest and with a smug, satisfied grin proclaim, 'Marvellous!' On the other hand, you might want to add some more effects, a commentary, incidental music, theme music or general ambient sounds.

Tape Formats and Sound Editing

Part of the complexity of sound editing is due to the fact that sound is recorded on to video tape in one of three ways – using the same part of the tape as the picture; a different part of the tape to the picture; or a combination of both. The part of the tape that sound is recorded on is known as a 'track'.

If you use any version of VHS camcorder (i.e. VHS, VHS-C, Super VHS or Super VHS-C) and it's got an 'Audio Dub' facility (check your handbook) then you're on easy street. With this you can record a new sound track directly on to the tape without affecting the existing picture. The only problem with this is that the new sound will completely replace the old.

If you try and dub new sounds on to Hi8 and 8mm tapes you'll also record over your existing picture – be warned!

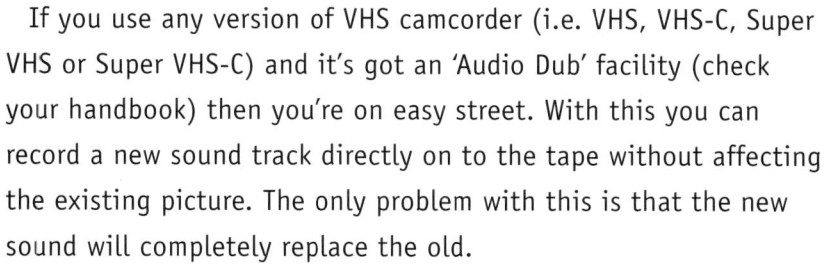

Beadle Tip

I'VE SAID IT BEFORE AND I'LL SAY IT AGAIN: IF IN DOUBT OVER WHAT TO DO, CONSULT YOUR CAMCORDER HANDBOOK. IT MIGHT BE LONG AND FULL OF PIDGIN ENGLISH PHRASES OFFERING YOU 'MULTITUDINOUS THANKS FOR BUYING MOST SOPHISTICATED PIECE OF VIDEO TECHNOLOGICAL EXCELLENCE' BUT IT COULD MAKE THE DIFFERENCE BETWEEN SUCCESSFULLY DUBBING NEW SOUND OR LOSING YOUR ORIGINAL PICTURE ALTOGETHER. TO BE ON THE SAFE SIDE, ALWAYS EDIT USING A COPY OF THE ORIGINAL TAPE (THIS APPLIES TO PICTURE AND SOUND EDITING). THIS MEANS THAT IF YOU DO MAKE MISTAKES – LIKE ERASING SOMETHING YOU SHOULDN'T – YOU CAN ALWAYS START AGAIN.

How Sound Is Added

This isn't a technical book so I'll just outline the basic principles behind adding new sounds to an existing sound track:

★Connect a VCR containing your edited video to another VCR via a sound mixer.

★The sound mixer, as its name cleverly suggests, is used to combine your existing sound track with sounds from different sources, for example, a cassette tape, CD, mini-disc, a record.

★Begin copying the edited video from VCR to VCR, watching it on a TV set.

★At the appropriate moment, play in the new sounds, taking your cue from the action you're watching on the TV.

★The VCR that's recording will end up with a second generation tape containing the edited video and its original sound track, but with the new sounds added in the appropriate positions.

★What more do you want?

Beadle Tips

★THROUGHOUT THE PROCESS REMEMBER TO MONITOR THE SOUND USING HEADPHONES.

★IT'S QUITE TRICKY MIXING SOUNDS IN YOURSELF AND IT'S FAR BETTER TO USE AN ASSISTANT. ONE OF YOU SHOULD WATCH THE PICTURE WHILE THE OTHER PLAYS IN THE DIFFERENT NEW SOUNDS AND MIXES THEM AS REQUIRED.

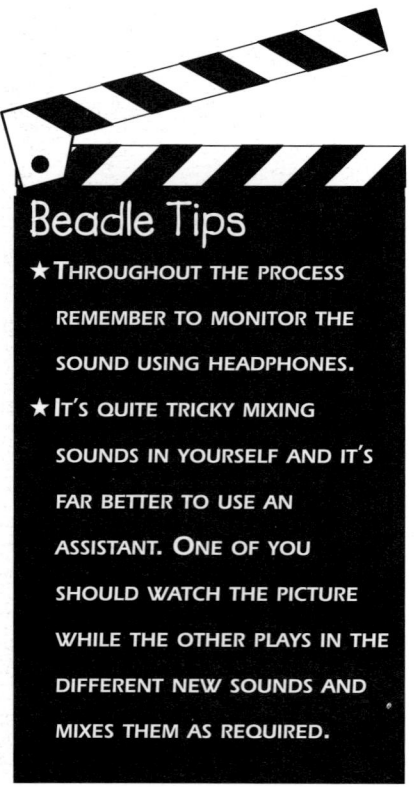

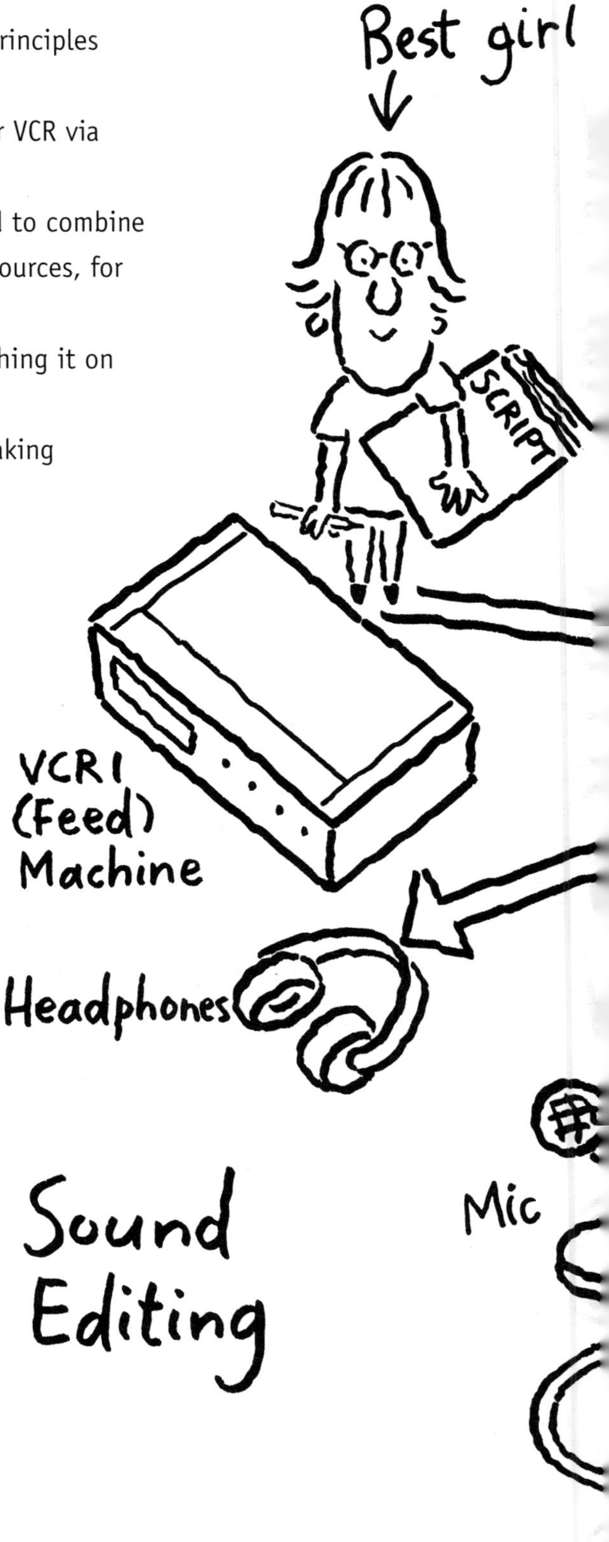

Best girl

VCR1 (Feed) Machine

Headphones

Sound Editing

Mic

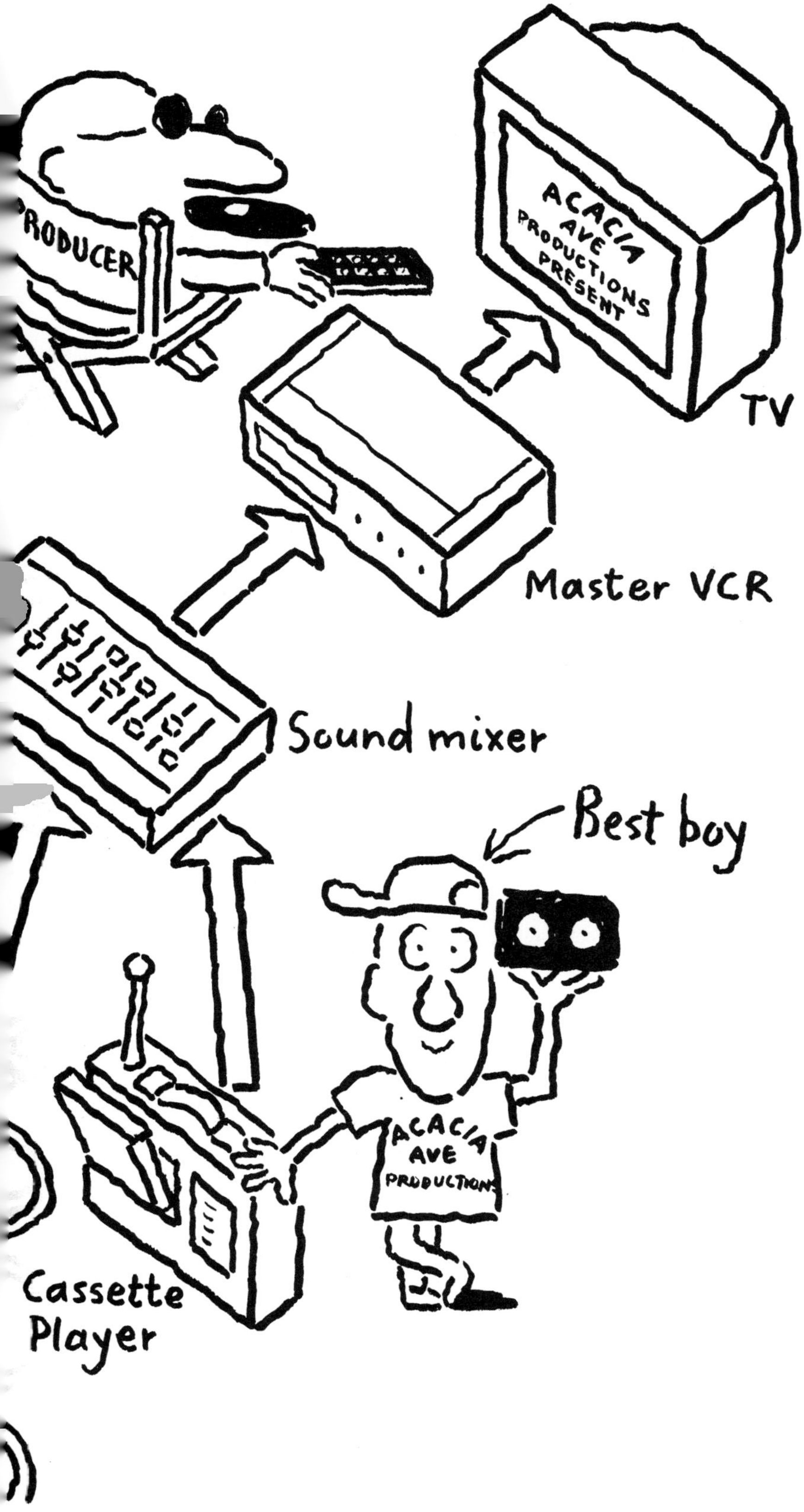

PRODUCER

ACACIA
AVE
PRODUCTIONS
PRESENT

TV

Master VCR

Sound mixer

Best boy

Cassette
Player

Beadle Tips

ADDING MUSIC OR SOUND
EFFECTS DURING EDITING CAN
HELP TO MAKE A 'STRAIGHT'
SCENE FUNNY.

SOME EXAMPLES INCLUDE:

★ ANIMAL SOUNDS PLAYED OVER
  A CHILDREN'S TEA PARTY

★ A MACHINE-GUN SOUND
  EFFECT PLAYED OVER A WATER
  PISTOL FIGHT

★ HEAVY SNORING PLAYED
  OVER A PARTICULARLY DULL
  WEDDING SPEECH

★ A LION ROARING WHEN YOUR
  KITTEN SAYS 'MIAOW'

★ STEPPENWOLF'S 'BORN TO BE
  WILD' PLAYED OVER SHOTS OF
  TWO OLD LADIES WALKING
  DOWN THE STREET WITH THEIR
  SHOPPING TROLLEYS.

USE YOUR IMAGINATION!

Holding Your Own Public Screening

The pay-off to everyone's hard work on your Blockbuster is the Official Screening, when you get to unveil the finished version. It's a party, a chance to say thank you and a guaranteed audience for your video. You *have* to hold one.

Your Screening

It's the big night – the first official screening of your Blockbuster. You've invited all the cast and crew around to your house, together with their families and people who weren't involved but who always bring a decent bottle to parties.

You let the excitement build, then you make your speech, thanking everyone for their hard work – and mercilessly teasing Uncle Fred for not being able to keep his dentures in place during the love scenes.

Now the lights go down. There is an excited hubbub which falls away to silence as your Blockbuster appears on screen. It's a hit! The audience laugh! They point at things. They go 'Ahhhh!' whenever your cat or your little daughter appears on screen. Your punchline brings the house down and there's thunderous applause as the closing credits roll.

They loved it! All that hard work you put in paid off. You feel great! Now you know what it's like to be Steven Spielberg!

There'll be calls to show it again. This time they'll enjoy it even more than the first time and they'll see all the little details you put in.

You feel on top of the world . . .

The trouble is, it's still only half past eight. The bowls of pretzels are still three-quarters full and only grandad has managed to get drunk yet. (Your mate Brian doesn't count because he was drunk when he arrived.) Everyone wants more. No one wants to go home. So how do you make a full evening of your screening?

Out takes etc.

As I mentioned earlier, you should keep your out takes and screen the best after you've shown your Blockbuster. Chances are, they'll bring the house down!

Left: Nana Julie receives the coveted 'Golden Kleenex of Montreux' award for 'Best Sandwiches and Iced Fancies Fed to a Hungry Cast and Crew'

Awards ceremonies

Hold your own Oscars. Give out little prizes or certificates for 'Biggest Ham', 'Most Number of Takes to Get it Right', 'Best Bucket of Water Over The Head' or whatever.

You should have awards for the crew as well, like 'Best Sound', 'Best Lighting' and 'Person who had to carry all the heavy equipment and didn't complain – much'.

Insist that everyone makes a speech – and make sure that everyone gets at least one award! (Use your new prop-making skills which you've learned from this book to make the actual awards – toilet rolls covered in silver foil and mounted on a small Variety pack of cereal will do fine.)

Earlier blockbusters

If this isn't your first video, you can screen others you've made too.

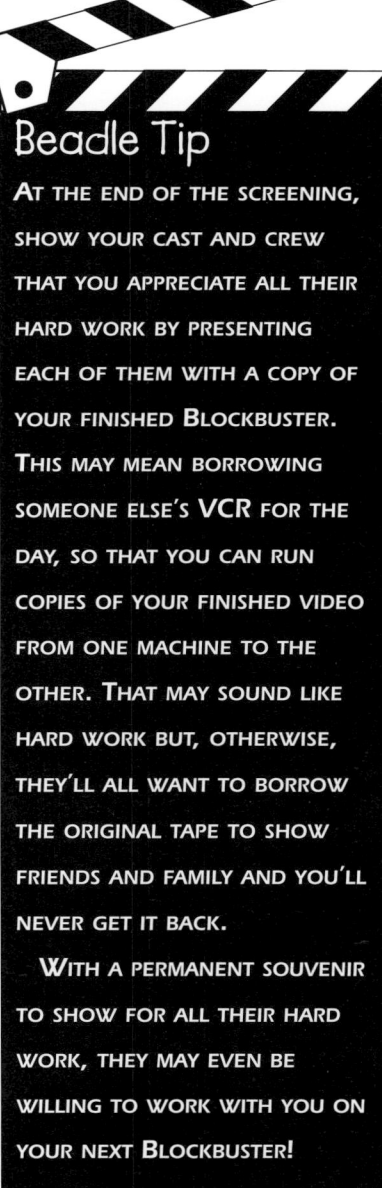

Beadle Tip

AT THE END OF THE SCREENING, SHOW YOUR CAST AND CREW THAT YOU APPRECIATE ALL THEIR HARD WORK BY PRESENTING EACH OF THEM WITH A COPY OF YOUR FINISHED BLOCKBUSTER. THIS MAY MEAN BORROWING SOMEONE ELSE'S VCR FOR THE DAY, SO THAT YOU CAN RUN COPIES OF YOUR FINISHED VIDEO FROM ONE MACHINE TO THE OTHER. THAT MAY SOUND LIKE HARD WORK BUT, OTHERWISE, THEY'LL ALL WANT TO BORROW THE ORIGINAL TAPE TO SHOW FRIENDS AND FAMILY AND YOU'LL NEVER GET IT BACK.

WITH A PERMANENT SOUVENIR TO SHOW FOR ALL THEIR HARD WORK, THEY MAY EVEN BE WILLING TO WORK WITH YOU ON YOUR NEXT BLOCKBUSTER!

Appendix 1 – Upgrading Your Camcorder

Who knows, after your first few comedy Blockbusters you might have got seriously bitten by the video bug and decide that your vintage Betamax camcorder the size of a vacuum cleaner really needs to go. This section isn't about the pros and cons of tape formats or the features found on specific makes and models. Let the staff in the high street shops tell you that. After all, that's what they're there for (apart from asking 'Do you need any assistance?' every eight seconds).

No. Here I'm going to give you some more fundamental hints and tips about choosing a new camcorder.

★Buy a few specialist video magazines and see which camcorders get good and bad reviews. The reviewers know far more than those spotty herbert Saturday shop boys.

★Be aware that expensive doesn't always mean best. Some low price camcorders are great - and some high priced models are real stinkers. Be guided by the expert opinions in the magazines, decide which one is right for you and phone around to see who stocks it locally. Be prepared to travel - or to wait - to get the camcorder you want.

★Even when you think you've decided on the right camcorder for you, always try out a few different ones before you decide which one to buy. You may find the viewfinder doesn't suit your eyesight, or the controls are awkward for your fingers to reach. See if you can hold it steady comfortably.

★While you're testing the camera, be sure to check the sound quality as well. Listen for clarity on audio playback - and be especially sure to listen out for motor noise. Some badly-designed camcorders will pick up the drone of the motor through the microphone, which is a serious fault. You'll find this on both expensive and low cost camcorders - so check before you buy!

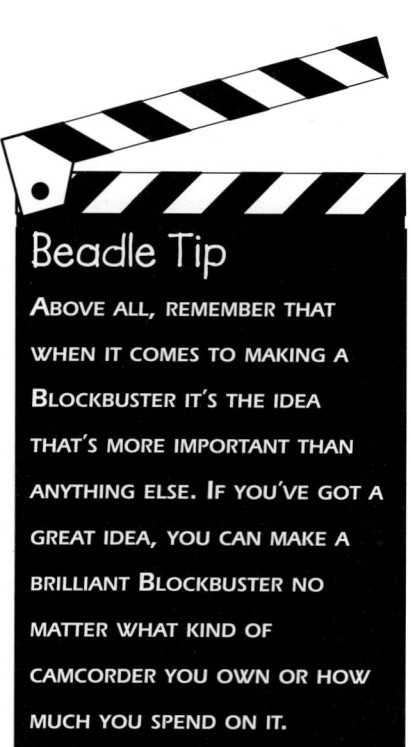

Beadle Tip

ABOVE ALL, REMEMBER THAT WHEN IT COMES TO MAKING A BLOCKBUSTER IT'S THE IDEA THAT'S MORE IMPORTANT THAN ANYTHING ELSE. IF YOU'VE GOT A GREAT IDEA, YOU CAN MAKE A BRILLIANT BLOCKBUSTER NO MATTER WHAT KIND OF CAMCORDER YOU OWN OR HOW MUCH YOU SPEND ON IT.

Appendix 2 — One Essential Accessory

Tripods

A tripod is vital. Remember that the biggest advance in camera technology in recent times has been the 'Steadicam'. No one wanted to buy the 'Unsteadicam', the 'WibblyWobblyCam' or the 'JerkyCam 2000'. Shaky pictures make the audience edgy, then increasingly nauseous. They also look very amateur.

Amateur video-makers want to act like professionals in all ways but one. They want to direct like pros, shoot like pros, edit like pros, get paid like pros - but do they want to use a tripod like pros? Do they heck!

I know tripods are awkward to carry around. I know they're inconvenient to keep setting up. I've kicked them. I've cursed them. I've fallen over them. But just remember one of Beadle's little tips: tripods might be heavy - but when it comes to getting good results, they're worth their weight in gold. Why? I'll tell you.

★Reason 1: As camcorders get smaller they get lighter. With less mass they're more prone to camera shake and what does camera shake mean? Wobbly pictures.

★Reason 2: The longer the focal length of your lens, the more magnified camera shake will be. This means that if you're at the telephoto extent of your zoom lens, the slightest movement of the camcorder will be exaggerated ten-fold (or more) at the lens. As camera zoom lenses get more powerful, the chances of camera shake are worsened.

★Reason 3: For panning, tilting, tracking and zooming to be effective, these moves have to be jerk-free (that's jerk as in movement, not jerk as in the camcorder operator). Only a tripod can give you the smoothness and fluidity needed for these camera moves.

★Reason 4: (Not as important as the other three but then again, not to be sneezed at, either.) Using a tripod will not only make you look like a pro - it will hopefully also get you thinking like one too, i.e. you'll be inclined to take more time in setting up shots and try different camera moves.

WHAT TYPE OF TRIPOD SHOULD I USE?

IDEALLY, ONE WITH THREE LEGS! SORRY, COULDN'T RESIST THAT. BUT SERIOUSLY, THERE'S NO POINT GOING FOR A TRIPOD THAT'S TOO LIGHT AND SPINDLY. IT MIGHT BE EASIER TO CARRY AROUND BUT YOU'LL BE NO BETTER OFF. CHECK THAT THE TRIPOD REACHES AT LEAST EYE-LEVEL, AND THAT THE LEGS CAN BE SPLAYED QUITE WIDE TO ACCOMMODATE LOW-ANGLE SHOTS.

YOU WANT A TRIPOD WITH BEEFY LEGS, THE THICKER THE BETTER, WITH BRACING STRUTS CONNECTING THEM TO THE CENTRE COLUMN. THOSE DESIGNED FOR 35MM STILL CAMERAS WILL INVARIABLY BE TOO LIGHTWEIGHT AND NOT DESIGNED FOR THE MOVES YOU'LL WANT TO MAKE WITH YOUR CAMCORDER.

THE MAIN COMPONENTS OF A TRIPOD ARE THE LEGS (OBVIOUSLY), A HEIGHT-ADJUSTABLE CENTRE COLUMN, AND THE PAN & TILT HEAD. THIS IS THE CHUNKY METAL BIT THAT ROTATES AND TILTS - WHICH YOUR CAMCORDER MOUNTS ON. THE MORE YOU PAY FOR A TRIPOD, THE BETTER QUALITY THE PAN & TILT HEAD IS - AND THE SMOOTHER THE MOVEMENT WILL BE.

Appendix 3 — Animation

Some of you might fancy yourselves as the creators of the next Wallace & Gromit but before you invest in an industrial-size pack of Plasticine remember that animation is very tricky on video. You need the right kind of camcorder - and the right kind of temperament!

Beadle Tip

IF YOU'RE ANIMATING SOMETHING, ALWAYS SHOOT IT UNDER ARTIFICIAL LIGHT. THAT WAY YOU CAN KEEP THE LIGHT CONSTANT ACROSS A SEQUENCE WITHOUT WORRYING ABOUT THE ROOM'S NATURAL LIGHT CHANGING AS THE SUN GOES BEHIND A CLOUD ETC.

It's a long fiddly process to create even a few seconds worth of video. Unfortunately, film is the ideal medium for animation - because film is a series of frames. All right, so technically video is also a series of frames or 'fields' or whatever you want to call them, but the vast majority of camcorders aren't designed to allow you to shoot a frame or even a few frames at a time. What you need is a camcorder with a 'Time-Lapse' facility but even these won't offer you very much in the way of flexibility.

If you do want to create a totally animated Blockbuster, cartoons are probably out of the question unless you're a good illustrator, but you can animate models, toys and everyday household objects to create a unique little Blockbuster. Consider ideas like these:

★The Adventures of Plasticine Man

★The day my shoes came to life

★War of the Kitchen Utensils

★Boxroom of Mystery - what do your child's toys get up to when she's out at school?

★Action Man and Barbi in 'Beware The Driller-Killer '

★'Dresser From Beyond' - the dressing table possessed by an evil spirit which talks by opening and shutting a drawer...

Other Uses of Animation

★ Poltergeist effects - objects seeming to move by themselves

★ Speeding things up - for example a family wolfing down a dinner

★ Dracula decomposing - changing the make-up slightly between takes. Buy your actor a beer for his patience!

Find Out More!

I hope this book has whetted your appetite to go out and make a fun video. If you're interested in learning more and developing your skills, why not read up on techniques and technicalities from the following excellent publications:

Books

Directing on Camera by Harris Watts (Aavo Media)

Chambers Film & TV Handbook (Chambers)

The Complete Video Course by Keith Brookes (Boxtree)

Video: A Complete Introductory Guide by John Hedgecoe
 (Mitchell Beazley)

The Camcorder User's Handbook by Peter Davison (Boxtree)

The Home Video Handbook by Stuart Dollin (Chancellor Press)

The Camcorder Handbook by Malcolm Squires (Headline)

The Complete Book of Video by David Cheshire (Dorling Kindersley)

Taking Better Videos (Cassell)

The Camcorder User's Video Handbook by Peter Davison (Boxtree)

Camcorder by Steve Parker (HarperCollins)

Camcorder Question & Answers by Steve Parker (HarperCollins)

The Complete Home Video Director by David Owen (Foulsham)

Getting the Best From Your Camcorder by Norman Tozer (Regency House)

Learn to Video in a Weekend by Roland Lewis (Dorling Kindersley)

The Video Maker's Handbook by Ian Graham (Octopus)

The Video Maker's Handbook by Roland Lewis (Marshall Editions)

Magazines

Camcorder User & Desktop Video

What Camcorder

Video Camera

Video World

What Video & TV

Video Clubs

Up and down the country there are hundreds of amateur video clubs. These guys tend to be very good and very professional – but they understand that everyone has to start somewhere, because they had to learn too. If you really want to improve your skills and do more ambitious Blockbusters, you should join a club.

Ask in your local library for details of any local clubs or write to one of the magazines, telling them where you live, and see if they know of a group near you.

The authors

The authors would like to thank the
following for their invaluable help and assistance:
Bonnie Beadle; Cassie Beadle; Cally the golden retriever; China the semi-bald cat;
Terry Carter; Liz and Jeff Davis; Luke Davis; Rob Ewen; Nigel Forsyth; Julie Hall;
Rebecca Hammerton; Andrea Hatton; Mary and Dennis Hatton; Philippa and Gage Hatton-Lepine;
Chris Jones at Computer Maintenance UK Ltd (Thames Ditton); Michael, Gill and Neville Landau;
Debbie, Polly and Barney Leigh; Philip and Edith Leigh; Alison MacLeod; Judy Martin;
Lindsay Symons; Graham Webb; Victoria, Elizabeth and Trevor Williamson;
Lesley Willis at Lightbox Creative Services